ZION OFFRAMP
51–100
(asemic dub)

Also by Mark Scroggins:

Poetry

obelisk absinthe: Zion Offramp 113–118
forage acanthus
Pest: Zion Offramp 65–70
Zion Offramp 1–50
Damage: Poems 1988–2022
Elegiac Verses
Pressure Dressing
Red Arcadia
Torture Garden: Naked City Pastorelles
Anarchy
Bodhrán Songs/Eight Poems (with E. A. Miller)

Prose

Arcane Pleasures: On Poetry and Some Other Arts
The Mathematical Sublime: Writing About Poetry
Michael Moorcock: Fantasy, Fiction and the World's Pain
Intricate Thicket: Reading Late Modernist Poetries
The Poem of a Life: A Biography of Louis Zukofsky
Louis Zukofsky and the Poetry of Knowledge

Edited

The Uncollected Louis Zukofsky: Poetry, Drama, Prose (with Jeffrey Twitchell-Waas)
Our Lady of Pain: Poems of Eros and Perversion by Algernon Charles Swinburne
"Additional Prose" in *Prepositions+: The Collected Critical Essays of Louis Zukofsky*
Upper Limit Music: The Writing of Louis Zukofsky

Praise for *Zion Offramp 51–100*

asemic dub—so Mark Scroggins subtitles *Zion Offramp 51–100*. Asemic language wants to say the unsayable, can't be deciphered with any certainty. The reader can only wonder, imagine, examine the choices the text proposes. To dub is to echo, to alter, to name, to arm. *asemic dub*, then. To name or imagine into being? To echo or rework, remake what happens? To arm the word, to make it mean? To baptize with language—is that substance or spirit? Scroggins is a Deacon of the heretical faith we call the world, a celebrant of its arcane and familiar particulars, its *heart-sunk, guarded privacies*. "Deacon" from the Greek, meaning servant, messenger, minister. On his altar lie all the world's tales and trash, its wounds and laws, lullabies and betrayals, plagues, pleasures, prophecies, memories, original sins, mutable histories, breathtaking weather, *vagrant blossoms*, birds and insects, *secrets in flames … ruining the work of time*. Ruining time itself, it seems, till we are utterly here. Only, where is here? Scroggins shows us how, though we are lost, benighted knights, we can read, think and feel our way along. And we can sing. *The words step forward, upright and healthy: / puella, girl; agricola, farmer; filia, / daughter. Simple, musical, sensuous.* I want to say, real. But not simple, not really. *Language like a subtle complex / tapestry Morris Persian labyrinthine daedalian.* Deacon Scroggins reminds us that words have the power to suffer for us, to bless and redeem us. What has been *spoken in darkness / shall be published in the light*. Strangely, the book seems not to end, not because Scroggins has promised a third volume of *Zion Offramp*, but because the poem feels magically contiguous with the world. It just keeps going. *Something happened*, something is happening, something may happen next, *a giant story / that tells all the stories the book / didn't tell. An endless book, spilling / over*, the mysterious, recurring *girl in her room … already a woman … passing under the Bridge of Sighs*.

—Billie Chernicoff

Praise for *Zion Offramp 1–50*

Zion Offramp is one of the most compelling, absorbing, and powerful books of American poetry to be published in some years. Hugely ambitious, mingling irony with wistfulness, and throughout richly, wittily, wickedly lyrical, it draws a road map through the dissonance and minor sublimities of daily mortal life, doing what poetry does best: building a negentropic machine against loss. It is not to be missed.

—Patrick Pritchett

What might there be beyond Zion, that once ultimate endpoint, that destination stop still resonant with righteousness and redemption? Or are we, more immediately, just fleeing Babylon? Endpoints. Wrong turns. Upended quests. All these, and dauntless conviction, haunt the fifty sections of Mark Scroggins's extraordinary new book length demi-poem, the first tranche of his long song, *Zion Offramp*, a serial poem periodically devastated by all that eschatology once and might yet still mean.

—Joseph Donahue

These are our *Cantos*—if Pound were with us today, if he hadn't gone off the deep end, and if he had managed to make it cohere just a little bit more.

—Norman Finkelstein

ZION OFFRAMP
51–100
(asemic dub)

Mark Scroggins

MadHat Press
Cheshire, Massachusetts

MadHat Press
MadHat Incorporated
PO Box 422, Cheshire, MA 01225

The Library of Congress has assigned
this edition a Control Number of
2025944832

ISBN 978-1-968422-03-5 (paperback)

Text by Mark Scroggins
Book design by MadHat Press
Cover image: *The Day Dream* (sketch)
by Dante Gabriel Rossetti
Author photo by Zach Barocas

www.madhat-press.com

First Printing

Printed in the United States of America

I knowe more than Apollo,
For oft, when hee ly's sleeping,
I see the starres att bloudie warres
In the wounded welkin weeping;
The moone embrace her shepheard,
And the Queen of Love her warryor,
While the first doth horne the star of morne
And the next the heavenly Farrier.

—"Tom o' Bedlam's Song," anonymous 16th–17th century

So I went vnto the Angel, & said to him, Giue me the litle boke. And he said vnto me, Take it & eat it vp, and it shal make thy bellie bitter, but it shalbe in thy mouth as swete as honie. Then I toke the litel boke out of the Angels hand, and ate it vp, and it was in my mouth as swete as honie, but when I had eaten it, my bellie was bitter.

—Revelation 10.9–10 (Geneva Bible, 1560)

51.

A locked box, a withheld
document. The spire danced
in flames, we feared the whole
fabric, labor of generations,
was ashing to the ground—
fate or accident or random
something ruining the work of time.
The book on the table Moorcock's
Firing the Cathedral—meaning of course
the Twin Towers. The video
on our phones the real thing.
Someone—up in that airless vault,
caged among the spider-work
of nine-hundred-year-seasoned
timbers—was burning papers,
feeding heart-sunk, guarded privacies
into a slowly growing flame.

Is it a secret you're holding? We all
have them, hoarded jealously close.
What you have spoken in darkness
shall be published in the light.

Calypso, the veiled one, holding
Odysseus close to her breast, soft
heart of her sunny island: *Apocalypse*,
unveiling when all secrets

are turned out like little boys'
grubby pockets. Nothing is hid
that shall not be made manifest.
Time is, time was, shall be no more.

A veiled sun fumbles behind
moving clouds, muffled
bassline in an especially muddy

mix. Did it ever really mean
anything, time passing?
The tree shagged with needles

breaks the light. Off east,
they stubbornly grow, are
cut down, digested and

metamorphosed into wrapping for
our purchased lives. How long a pine
lives is anyone's guess. Last summer

I saw trees—huddled, spectacularly
gnarled—that had stood
aloof while men gnawed

themselves to ribbons at Edgehill
and Naseby. I was not there.
Feathers, ribbons, leather in the mud.

And what did it mean, to be about
        his father's business?
The hand was already upon us
down there. Corrugated aluminum,
glass splinters across the sand.
He spoke, that is, as one having
authority. To loose or bind.
        You've got some skills, she said
in the half-light. Held it to myself,
jealous, riven by failure, dreamed
about it for days afterward.

"image of the people" gasping
weeping holding cell phones
aloft to capture it all
the emptied isle

Then one day you came
to the end of the maze's
        last unexplored
        passage, the turn
of the labyrinth that had
to be its ending, or its
        center, or at least a bridge
        to some new tangle
of paths, and found
only a blank wall.
        A night like
        so many others, air

cold and clear, noises
on the breeze. You knew
        it might be a night
        like no other, real
self-knowledge, abasement
and abjection and utter
        unalloyed abnegation.
        Maybe tonight, maybe
here and now, again
and again amen.

52.

Bring out the trumpets, the lyre!
Does the cardinal, alit on the grass,
know how red he blazes? Seal and assurance
of a late spring, with the duller robin
an arm's-length away. High diction
        for a low mood. He read
the obituaries first these days, calculating
birth and death dates against
his own. I try to cultivate a steady
hand, gaze in idiot
        wonder at pages darkened
and illuminated with precise,
infinitely repeated strokes. The light here
is green. Blue trumpets, green lyre.

The moon was orange rust
and fading fast, but no not
        threatening, just strange—
and she arched herself back
on that hardwood floor,
        reaching out her arms
in invitation. Fading fast,
all wild and acrid and strangely
        drunk, a hair between
my teeth, our cries clouding
out the rusty orange moon.

Spring never took us unawares upstate:
the descent of the birds, chattering

from before dawn, dazed rabbits
wandering newly alert across the backyard
grass: after days and weeks
of low drizzle and chill grey skies
the sun bursting out close, triumphant
and permanent. Morning like a shiny
Amazon package on the doorstep.

Light of the quad through
        the window-blind the only
light, the disc-changer changing
        from Roxy's *Avalon* to Marvin's
Let's Get It On—the ashy smell
        of Keith's cigarettes and Drexel's
endless milky teas, still
        tangled damp in the bedsheets.

        Prosthetic vision. A Venus reclines
        full-length asleep, one hand
        cupping her *mons pubis*. Cupid
        threads his mother's nipple
        between nimble fingers.
        Patches of forsythia ignite
        across the Park, the magnolia
        over the driveway has begun
        pinking out. Two weeks ago
        I met a painter bemoaning—
        like everyone else—obscurity.
        He was talking *representation*,

truth. He would set the curve
of a student's breast against
a pastel skyline, tangle
of his own prophetic beard
against the afternoon light.
Painting is elegy for things seen.

And that photograph: in profile, her aquiline
nose, eyes deliberately closed—hair flecked
with premature grey. The quad beyond
is white with snow, snow frosting
the bushes, snow shelving off
the evergreens. Bronzino's vision
in the *Allegory* was blunted
for generations—a spray
of leaves to soften Cupid's
provocative bum, unlikely
coil of drapery over the goddess's sex.
The nipple between his fingers
was painted over, painted over
his mother's tentative,
assertive tongue.

53. *Coriolanus Dub*

What is the city but the people?

common cry of curs dissentioned
rogues reek a' th' rotten fens quarter'd
slaves multitudinous tongue dead
carcasses of unburied men base slaves

Doomed and devoted, the hero
plays out the family drama
of his nobility, falls at the hands
of a manipulated "rabble."

The earliest records extant
date from two centuries later—
some historians consider him
a myth, like Numa Pompilius

King Saul or George Washington.
Parson Weems draws back the curtain
on a receding spectacle
whose farthest figures are mere

notations of shadow, scratches
on polished tusks. Scrimshaw,
like this, the off-duty time-
killer of becalmed sailors.

The tales of the old times have come down
to us in various forms, through many hands,

over many many years. Some versions
bear no resemblance one to another.
Some are in verse, some in ornate prose, others
in rough, staccato outline. Still others only
scattered notes. Dates and locations disagree.
Proper names have evolved, have been changed.
Several central figures have dropped out
of the record entirely, while some versions
introduce wholly new heroines, villains.

I twist the volume to half, the gain
all the way up, so the notes
        emerge with an edge
of strain, aggravated, tense—
the grand gesture, the melodramatic
dissonance, sudden cloudburst—
but the delicate turn of light
        on a single leaf, hastened
across the marble floor
        by an opened door's
surprise gust—beyond
me, like the inking
        of those precise ivory
tablets—what the birds make
outside the window, across
        the avenue and over the traffic,
isn't exactly *melody*, but musical
nonetheless—an ostinato
        minimalist, atonal even

The editor is hard at work, trying
to establish a reliable, received text
out of a midden of incompatible *Handschrift*.
Names must be standardized, chronologies
established and coordinated, sequences
of cause and effect sorted properly out.
Corners must be cut; Gordian knots
of conflicting reference must be severed
with the sword of informed conjecture—
guesswork, civilians call it.

At full volume, the windows rattle
and the tchotchkes dance
        across the bookshelves.
The glass doors of that bookcase
rattle too, but the volumes inside
        slumber undisturbed: notebooks,
datebooks, laundry lists and drafts.
Nowhere the unique copy of the ur-text,
        teleological apotheosis of heroic
        editorial labor. The book
        has never existed. Does not yet
        exist. The hero plays out his family
        agon in the space between redaction
        and emendation, where the dust-motes
        tremble, dance ecstatically
        on the waves of magnetic,
        mesmeric dub. No birds sing.

54.

Every earthquake ends up
in a museum. Revolution turns
into style, in the vulgar sense.
The drizzle so light
it seems to drift down
against the dark of the trees,
and the chainsaw falls
intermittently silent.
I wanted to cede the initiative
to color, let the line take
its own walk. I wanted
to give the horse
its head, the coffee-grounds
pile up, dry, and sift down
through the strata of discards.
It all piles steadily up,
sorting's a thing you do
on a weekly basis, or when
you remember. The museum
of earthquakes, of wars,
of repeated and futile
activities. You could make
a life's work of paging
through those stacks and boxes,
dribbling out leaks, communiqués
to an always-eager fanbase.
The museum of earthquakes
shifts from gallery to gallery,
we were never sure what

to expect when we crossed
another threshold. The floors
are canted at unexpected
angles, adjusted day to day.
The gallery plan is always
out of date—like the maps
punctuating the walls, provinces
of pink or kelly green contracting
and expanding like some playful
cephalopod. Only artifacts
        can nail down the past, assign
        it a proper author or provenance.
Here is a fragment of Orpheus'
lute, washed ashore a bit down
        the coast. And here a swatch
        of Sappho's holiday chiton,
brighter terracotta than we'd expected,
hem embroidered with a simple Greek key,
        chest intricate with figures
        light and dark, *poikilos*, a Möbius-
                strip of red-figure movement—
                dancers, harvesters, sportsmen,
        warrior, girls with lyres, flowers
        in their hair, erotic pursuits beneath
                dappled tree-shadow, archaic
                amphora or Wedgewood urn:
Winckelmann's or Flaxman's Hellas—
the catalogue is always incomplete.

Outside the insects roar
like a bank of document-
shredders, and you're encouraged
to recycle the little metal badge
validating your right to be
where you are. Artifacts
behind shatterproof glass, the holograph
letters on display in a quaint
vitrine: they underwrite our purpose,
our much-asserted direction.
Hey hey, the bartender says, polishing
the inevitable tumbler, and pours us
a glass of the local favorite.
Licensed and vaccinated,
we run in circles around the dusty
fenceline, sniff each others' behinds
in greeting or enquiry.

55.

That's enough, she said, time
to stop ducking into galleries
and sauntering through museums,
time to pack up the car
and head west, north, anywhere
away from the forecast cone.
Careful with that plywood, son,
and mind the corrugated
aluminum. Hatches
must be battened down—
securely this time. All night
we heard the wind gnawing
around the doors, fumbling
at the unshuttered windows.
We drove all day, a grey wall
of rain and twisted air
at our heels. Lana Del Rey
was on the sound system,
and Sly and the Family
Stone—Brooklyn baby,
in a family affair. If *I*,
I reflected, *is an other*,
then *we* is yet another
still. Who is *we*, and how
did that club get started,
anyway? *Oui*, yes, *we*,
the I and its other, all in
the same boat, same subway
car, trash and papers

spiraling in its wake.
Is this all overheard?
does that make us all
eavesdroppers, peeping
Thomasinas and doubting
Thomases? That bit of Jimi's
Monterey Pop head-
stock, singed more than the cigarette-
burns on Eric's "Blackie," laid out
like a splinter of the True Cross—
but less convincing than a finger
in the actual incision. We saw it,
it appeared, a true performance
if on film: the guitar is never just
a guitar, you don't need Freud
to see that—but to kneel before
that instrument of desire, douse
and light it up—self-mutilation worthy
of Alcibiades defacing the herms,
or Origen's over-literal reading of Matthew's
gospel. The museum of the True
Cross, the museum of hurricanes,
museum of amber or polyurethane
in which our memories are fixed
so that strangers, card-carrying
members of *we*, can overhear
them. Time is frozen only
in artifacts, pauses in objects
photographs and made things.

Black hole of the tunnel
before us, storm at our heels.

56.

She's asking, over and again,
about the Law, what it allows
and forbids, enjoins and proscribes.
The idea of the Law—like the Word

in John—was there before
the Law itself. The Laws
agreed themselves before
they consented to be written down.

She's afraid of the Law. Afraid
the Law will follow her, pull her over
on the street. The Law will know
she made that turn without signaling.

The Law was written down on stone tablets,
then elaborated in volumes of commentary,
illustrations, and explanation. *You illustrate*
the moment before *or the moment* after

the event, someone said—*never the event*
itself. That bit I can't quite remember
from *The Wrecker,* when someone or other
jumps up—out of the blue—and stabs

someone else. I don't recall the event,
only how shocked I was to read it.
Tablets of stone, tablets of flesh.
In the "Penal Colony," the Law writes—

literally—on the subject's body,
as the tattooist scripts your lover's name
across your ribcage. She was once afraid
of needles—"just a pinch," they always say.

A god gave us the Law. A tall
and handsome white man clambered
down the mountain with it all
neatly written out, signed even.

Hammurabi, Solon, Moses midwifing
a new regime of order, tranquility.
On the fence's other side life is
nasty, furtive, solitary, brutish, short.

In the movie the "Lawgiver" is statuary:
a noble, portly orangutan, hieroglyphs
down the leather lapels of his
sweeping Second Empire coat.

White spots on the MRI. She knows
what a tumor looks like, at least,
and it's not that, at least. Open

suppurating wound, weeks after—
the blood wells into its scab
beneath the isinglass of superglue.

Enough about wounds, openings,
invasions. The wound and the Law.
The Law is health, enforced and ascetic.

The words step forward, upright and healthy:
puella, girl; *agricola*, farmer; *filia*,
daughter. Simple, musical, sensuous.

Combine them by the laws
of combination, of declension
and conjugation. Yoked together

like the flap of skin over a lopped
fingertip, glued down into forced
conjunction, healing, ascetic meld.

All extremities nicked and spotted,
freckled and otherwise discolored.
Law immaculate, without spot or stain.

Drinking champagne from the socket
        of a dead man's prosthesis; micro-
                dosing the tedium
of an unfixed weekend; the storm-cloud
        of last century passes over
                our sheds and villas, lintels
smeared with the blood
        of uncounted, unaccountable
                lambs and kids; the callus

wears away, the superglue powders
white and circles down
the drain. The "storm-cloud
of lust," I misread above. Lintels
smeared, still. Dub Pesach.
Passover dumbshow.

57. *The Virtue of Narrative*

There was, they were told in the meeting,
an informer among them—someone feeding
their names, their trade secrets, their clever
and subtle subterfuges, to the authorities.

Or to the press, the shop steward murmured,
her high forehead red in the torchlight,
her eyes dilated and darting fire.
We blanched at the words, looked uneasily

at comrades to our right and left,
behind and before us, shifted our weight
from foot to foot. Every detail
of the description was a cliché,

start to finish, the pace and rhythms
of the sentences and lines an imitation
of some book my grandparents might
have read, had they ever laid aside

their Bible after long days toiling
in the tobacco fields. *One of you,*
the Leader told us in a low voice, marks
of her upper incisors still visible

in her lower lip, a line of lipstick
rimming the bones of her sharp teeth,
will betray us yet again. We felt
betrayal in the sweat of our crotches,

the bristling backs of our necks, wet
jungles of our armpits, insistent erotic
itch of our nipples, roughened and chapped
by the coarse fabric of our shifts.

The torches, the manual has it,
must be held in wrought-iron brackets—
though some ambitious innovators
set them in the hands of disembodied arms,

thrusting from the walls like erections
through glory-holes—and the pronouncement
of betrayal must be accompanied
by a dark, minor-chord *obligato.*

Walls are always rough-hewn, floors
necessarily damp. There was an age
of clutter and abundance, then an age
of clean, antiseptic lines and spaces.

The narration is cluttered again, ripe
with crannies and kickshaws, erotic
if not fecund with abundance. But ironically.
Who could it be, we all asked, and were confused

when she said something—I didn't quite
catch it all—about *dipping a sop,*
handing it off to a *designated scapegoat.*
Oil of the offering glittered in the torchlight.

How many months did Holman Hunt bend
himself in the Levantine heat, cheeks and nose
peeling from the sun, to capture that infernal
goat? Its eyes, staring through matted hair,
speak to us, draw out pity. Dried spittle
clots the corners of Hunt's beard.
The landscape, in the event, swallowed
the animal, swallows the painter
in a maze of pinks and ochres
too vivid to be real. The Scapegoat
still stumbles across the dry seabed,
the Scapegoat's body, hanged
in self-disgust, has broken
from its gibbet and fallen down
the tumbled slope, spilling entrails
and apologies like a bride's train.

We loved to be betrayed,
        which meant that someone—
some Judas, some Quisling, someone
        with a face and name—
had actively caused us
        to be in the shit
                we woke up and found
        around our knees.
                We love to be betrayed
almost as much
        as it hurts to be

the betrayer. You stole
        that kiss among the parked
                cars behind the pub,
        that stoned, dreamy leer
                and grope in the pool
of a streetlamp. Better a bad conscience
        than no conscience at all.

The betrayal narrative
must be the oldest story
there is, the one you tell
your kids at bedtime
over the soft lullabies, the one
they repeat under their breaths
holding your fleshless hand
in the hospital chill, respirator
clicking and breathing,
as they watch the clock
and check their messages.

58.

What did the Founding Fathers mean
when they set those semi-legible symbols
in the rock, laid out those circles
of standing stones, opened the turf
to reveal that giant, chalk-white, ithyphallic
warrior? White Horse, they say,
is just a whiskey. There are old stories,
like old roads paved over, repeatedly
resurfaced, fitted
with exits and on-ramps and elaborate
signage, heading back into pasts
every bit as bright with the shimmer
of shipwreck as our own—*shipwreck*
or *new hope*, motifs we can't bear
to voice aloud. The bus we're on
swings wide at the corners, scrapes
the ice-sheathed twigs and branches.
The streets were laid out
for horses and buggies, before that
for rude wagons: the bus jostles
aside cars, bikes, hapless
pedestrians. The roadway is salted
white, wet in the corners, grey mounds
sulking from yesterday's snow-squall.
In one old story, they pulled down
the dictator's statue, hauling it over
with ropes and tackle, chanting
and cheering, only to find it brazen
hollow: his brawny thighs

and rounded barrel chest packed
with zip-tied coils of wire, loose
green circuit boards. They doused
his lithesome page-boys' hair
with brown Caribbean rum, tongued
the trickles from the curves
of their cheeks, set them alight.

They only hint at that story
in the big book, figure you've heard
it already by the fourth episode
of the new season. Revelation arrives

with some regularity anymore, enough
to pull my eyes back to the screen
when they've been wandering off
to the seldom-contemplated picture window.

The bus, you said, is really just a mass
of stories—and so is the street
it's sliding along. And how that transport
system comes to be what it is—evolves
or accretes or is built—comes to send
its glad tidings to the suburbs and outer
boroughs and clusters of ramshackle huts
out among the dark, hollow hills—
is maybe a *theological* question.

Did it grow over the decade and centuries
like a fabulous coral reef, revising its routes
against adverse currents, moving its way
        around boulders or sunken U-boats, city-large
        hulks of unremembered cruise ships,
        or did some carefully formed, expense-accounted
                cabal—if you were in their know
                you'd recognize their names—unveil
                each generation's dazzling, up-to-date,
bug-ridden iteration? Every bus behind schedule,
every metaphor fatally mixed. It bears us over

those every-shifting rivers by bridges or fords,
hauls us air-conditioned or sweating, open-windowed

surly, to our several unwritten
destinations. The tour guides gave us

a break yesterday—a sunny, chill afternoon—
and you and I rambled up the hill

to stroll among the standing stones,
to try to read what moss and erosion

hadn't rendered illegible of the flattened
markers of the last three or four reboots.

You filled a little notebook with decipherings—
I could read *Enoch Power*, I could read

I Get Knocked Down, I could read *Fuck*
the Police. There had been black mountains

off to the north, but they'd been knocked
down. Holes in the ground, between the chalk

and the turf, were stuffed with inexplicable
treasures, ancient shiny artifacts

and softly decaying offprints, inscribed
from one mage to another. The ground

beneath our feet—under the turf, under
the chalk, under the salting of melted

and splintered human ivory—was a midden
of papers and spongy bindings, rusted staples

and binder clips. Ash of newsprint
drifted down on us in the narrow street

when we ducked under the awning
of the kebab-seller's truck, torn pages

clung to the tires of the weary public
transit. The cathedral, straining its unfinished

head over Morningside Heights, was
burning and drowning at the same time.

59.

The Future Is Unwritten across
her right shoulder a circled
A on the other small
of the back a red
star downcast eyes when hailed

unfairly in retrospect shower curtain
masks the disabled washroom stall
rooms reeking faintly the words
spray out and fall to
the floor your ashen hair

Shulamith golden hair bits tangled
in quarter-century's memory Pierre smoking
in the doorway Krystyna smiles
as the St. Matthew Passion
drones in the background thirty

million out of work building
its way up from recession
so that the Boca library's
construction is delayed for lack
of Chinese cement a *goombah*

suit so shiny you could
see your face in it
twenty years pass over the
face shoulders curve and slump
morning light daylight artificial filtered

disavowed by joy or downcast
by miscarriage too many factors
twining cunning variable currents across
crossed wires tangled puppets dusty
and slumped as if disappointed

the picture-plane bisected diagonally upper
left Jesus the sun radiating
golden beams Beatrice encircled by
the moon lower right a
cloud of stars red-haired angel

steps forward front and center
read and eat the taste
was sweet but after sour
in the pit of my
belly left turn in heavy

traffic heavy rain emptied reclaimed
propane and CO_2 canisters brief
enchanting siren over the ridge
I shook his hand was
photographed with him a lifetime

ago eyes closed the procurator's
hands carefully washed the circumstance
and pomp panelling and richly
carved carpets leather polished oxblood
cufflinks lapel pins prose extruded

beyond the laws of rhetoric
Demosthenes' pebbles the rude pictograph
pointing a given aurochs fire
hill burst into song along
a line of melody succession

pricked out across moments air
dispersed almost immediately into gas
turkey carcass cooling on the
countertop Reddi-Wip nitrous oxide
dishes and implements slowed-down haze

crossed wires across variable currents
to transcend these sublunary arguments
realm of forms ideal laws
handed down like an unlikely
shaky torch no stone tablets

spark-shower hand of God in
Harryhausen stop-motion finger of fire
beards pasted on powder grey
1970s Victorian palpably different from
the millennial variety stubble sweat

and general reeking erotic tangibility
smell disappears from the later
works though food and tobacco
perdure versions of magical trail
mix home's cold cuts *versus*

airport's offerings the carbon tax
of getting here to there
sun hiding somewhere southward as
per usual it all falls
apart the whole puzzle continually

suspended on the point of
disintegration *The Future Is Unwritten*
overwritten pasts present not a
moving point or line but
a messy palimpsest spongy eggs

tentative ink over half-erased pencil
unwritten story toils forward recursively
do I repeat myself very
well then multitudes contain you
portrayed and repeated the fragrance

from a vanished immaterial bouquet
strewing petals like some Eleusinian
maiden blacksmithing red-hot fireplace implements
into true-love gatework beaten leaves
nature's curves mimic'd in grisaille

the outcome is baked in
if not precisely written foreseen
from a long way off
the two-miles' exit the merge
the hard but obligatory merge

moisture makes the air raw
to the touch eyelids skinned
back chapped fingers cuticles tender
asphalt darkened by moisture outlines
laid sharp and bare cutting

the fifty-years' seal opening sifting
another century's letters ceremoniously tossed
into the present's moral calculus
integral of attraction or default
voices called out or canceled

warring intestinal or internecine fumbled
zippers buttons hooks and eyes
a suavity beyond celluloid or
digital ten-fingered typing or secretarial
honors so often acknowledged last

humors of bile phlegm *soleil*
noir punting the Stygian river
lately relegated to the museum
of forbidden symbology broken gutter
angling off from garage roof

eye of green i'the pitiful
cold ordinary happiness an extraordinary
notion in days and endless
weeks of shock disbelief awe
and finger-eating chill heroes avatars

drop abruptly off the board
erase bits of one's childhood
unwritten future past utterly blank
now spreading like a stain
across tiles in every direction

red bleeds through the page
like deficits eating a rabbit
city lights diffused in clouds
tree limbs in midnight relief
the chosen constraints begin imperceptibly

to shape thought's channels random
only within random elective bounds
the commons we grazed on
Old Man of Coniston Founding
Fathers the Golden Bird and

somewhere beneath murky oceanic dub
bottom the One slipped away
fading disappearing without a bow
or acknowledgment you raised your
hopes again against reasonable hopes

knew it wouldn't work knew
it was no practical use
knew what made it impossible
emo boys send a plaintive
"heart" comment to golden girl's

Insta ringletted earth priestess poet
posts a pointed response volume
tongued to overdrive under purple
showers and deep raked hotel
liaisons what speak to speech

rostrum to break the uncreating
ice phlegm mucus and slippery
secretions crystallizing around our ankles
speech to speak as trumpets
as dull jazz bass octave-divided

dub tablas and ghatams fingers
supple and strong surprisingly soft
calluses washed away sanded smooth
by the clapping and counting
numbers off the charts unreadable

rhetoric of conversation pebbles around
the pool barbeque to raise
a laugh an eyebrow some
hint of connection or fellow-feeling
cars homes money interior design

I want syntax like rhizomes
not blocks branching threads netting
reticulated at irregular intervals not
piled like blocks or pebbles
stacked in lively durable impermanence

language like a subtle complex
tapestry Morris Persian labyrinthine daedalian
so the ear eye wander
directionless in all directions directed
distracted and diverted from thoroughfares

to byway which is now
thoroughfare alleys to shaded boulevards
which were interstates or Autobahns
their exits offramps merges transmogrified
and ramified and seamlessly joined

with the breathing throbbing network
overlapped intertwined coiled recoiled related
capillary rhizomatic make this meet
that *and* that and all
the others queer and unremarkable.

60. *Spinoza|Andy Gill*

You begin the treatise by defining
terms, nailing down denotations and slippery
connotations, eliminating ambiguities and clearing up
unfamiliar usages. You begin with a
capital letter, even an ornament. Maybe
a flower, an angel tangled in

vines or leafage, an animal biting
its own tail. Begin by counting
how many problems need solving, how
many words remaining before the end
of the chapter, of the page,
the line. There are six problems:

The first is substance, then attribute,
then mode. Begin with a point,
then a line. Middle C, without
sharps or flats. The scale is
artificial, the instrument can play any
note that exists. Hit the root

on the One is one way
to begin, the most canonically sanctioned,
but some authorities—venerated, even godlike—
prefer to descend or ascend from
the third or fifth. Begin with
an introduction, then strike it out.

An initial quiet watchfulness, wiped out
by a forceful statement of melody.
And the bad tidings wash in—
that dissonant scratching on the off-beat,
feedback and ironic, low-voiced mumblings against
power, will get you dead. Like

all of us, in the long
run. End it coughing and scratching,
off the beat, off key. End
it asleep in your own bed
or your lover's. It's the only
book, the treatise, you'll ever publish.

61. *The People of Tsīyōn*

Our ethnographers, embedded to the point
of identification, could trace out several
strands of continuity: word of mouth,
from elder to younger, and the living examples
of the former—however briefly they might
linger; written records, jealously
safeguarded and subject to periodic review
and wholesale revision, when necessary. The future
may be unwritten—that's not at all clear—
but the past can most certainly be revised.

Our informants, embedded to the point of
identification and absorption, offered no judgments
or practical advice, barely any analysis—
little more than raw data, however carefully
notated and categorized. Intertribal relations,
they observed, remained remarkably stable:
exogamous pairings ticked up a point or two
some years, then dipped back down; endogamy
continued the general rule of the road. Population
losses from occasional border skirmishes

were usually made good in a few seasons,
from postwar baby boomlets or influxes
of captives, soon absorbed into the population
at large. The subjects had no notion
of *race*, of *nation*, of any default relationship
beyond the extended family unit, itself
an ill-defined concept. They sorted individuals

not by physical traits—hair or eye color,
bodily proportions, skin tone—but by predominant
humor, favoring the sanguine and phlegmatic

over the splenetic or bilious. Their metaphysics
and theology proved frustratingly opaque,
though it's possible our informants' growing
embeddedness—their identification, their absorption—
made them strangely reluctant to set down
in writing what they might have been told,
might even have ultimately found themselves
assenting to. The subjects had no word
or concept for *human being* in general,
seeming to view themselves—and their gradually

assimilating observers—on a close continuum
with all other unrooted living beings, and on a
somewhat more distant continuum with the trees
and grasses, even the fungi and lichens.
They were frank and open, and if not exactly
welcoming—our informants were initially accepted
without ceremony or comment—they made no
sign at any point of concealing or holding back
whatever information our people sought.
Their islands are densely settled, but not

overpopulated. They regard the ruins left
by previous cultures with a kind of quizzical
indifference. Their sense of *time*, especially,

is of great interest, if extraordinarily difficult
to grasp. It absolves them of the fear of death—
needless to say their theology involves no
system of postmortem rewards or punishments—
and equips them with a curious equanimity
in the face of armed conflict or natural
disaster. One might call them *apathetically happy.*

62.

Don't know why, but before they
knew it they were counting again,
after all that time not worrying
about numbers, not keeping count.
How many telephone poles whipped by,
how many mile markers, how many
nights alone—counting might keep
things under control, make the wind
stop whipping through your hair,
the air stop eating away at
the edges of chrome excrescence,
the hood ornaments, the ship's
rostrum and the eye painted
greenly on the prow. It all passes
so quickly anymore. The chrome
consensus, stainless steel food
service surround. I throw one
thing after another, I lose
count, I stop counting, I
don't count anymore.

> Under the patio light the rat
> writhed and twitched, in labor
> maybe we thought clearly in pain.
> Its fur slick-dark, pasted down
> with sweat, hindquarters spasming.
> Maybe *the miracle of birth*, on herringbone
> Chicago brickwork, out by
> the pool—but no instead

a nasty bulging cyst beside
the wee thing's anus split open
and disgorged a thumbnail-sized
squirming larva, some fucking parasitic
botfly, like Sin springing full-formed
from Satan's migraine-head
in Milton, or Bacchus from Zeus'
ropey thigh, or Starbucks
muscling its shiny mermaid
form—all slick with birth-mucus—
from some steamy anal fistula—
all wet with mingled blood and pus—
on the regal backside of the Statue
of Liberty, crouched at difficult stool.

Dear —,

Yes, I know it's become the most weary cliché, sticking an epistolary passage in a poem, writing a poem as if it were a letter, stringing a bunch of the damned things together into some kind of festering garland or florilegium. But sometimes I just want to talk to someone, you know, another human being with a face and eyes and a hand that I could imagine reaching out to shake—like Paul Celan talks about somewhere.

The weather here is fine and sunny, I can hear mourning doves in the backyard. My eyes are probably deceiving me from here but I could swear that the pink magnolia is just about to bud. Some of the neighbors have snowdrops and crocuses across their lawns.

You weren't there this weekend, though I guess everyone expected you, and I wasn't there either, and if I'd been there I imagine I'd have lain down in that Tenderloin hotel room—the one I told you about, between the porn shop and the strip club—curled up on the bathroom tiles, all aqua and Seventies, and tried to weep.

I keep writing because you're dead and can't read this, or I'm dead and can't possibly put it in the mail, or maybe we're both dead, posthumous shades still walking around in our Eighties flip collars or our Nineties ripped flannels, looking in the store windows where nobody's moving, nothing's moving—not even the light—except for the receipt tapes in the cash registers.

Cliché upon cliché, then—that this is a letter at all, and then chat about the weather, which you know can't be relied on—everything I say, after all, is a lie—and then a rambly peroration on absence and the lack of communications, like some end-of-semester project from a state university film major, drunk on Pasolini and Jacques Derrida.

It's even in prose, this cliché-letter-poem, yet another cliché, as if in the pressure of getting my thoughts down on paper: imagine I'm sitting at a desk in a rented room, under a twenty-five-watt light bulb, pounding this out on a portable manual typewriter. A bottle of bourbon by my side, three-quarters empty.

I'd say *please write*, but I'm not writing this, much less sending it, and one or both of us is as I've explained dead.

I'm sorry I wasn't there when you needed me. I was there when you died, but you didn't know it, and I'd been away doing my own selfish things when you needed me before. Or I'm sorry I wasn't there when you died, that I'd run off years before out of sheer cowardice and selfishness when you needed me most. I know I let you down, and I can't forgive myself, and even if I was selfish and stupid enough to forgive myself, it's not my place to do the forgiving. And you can't forgive me because you're dead. And maybe I am too.

Love,

M

63.

Specters haunting the continent
this year, word has it. A deathly
virus, striking down old and young
alike, most readily spread at meetings
of poets and academics; the return
of the good old witch-hunt, peaked
paper hats, the ducking-stools
and *auto-da-fés*; the grand orgy
of purity and expedience fucking its way
to a mountainous climax on every large
and hand-held screen. We are
at sixes and sevens, prime and no-prime
that together make an ill-starred
table setting—have we given over
counting again?—and all the things
you learned once to your wonderment—the meaning
of Sussex, Essex, and Middlesex, the principles
by which they numbered the interstates—
so that you repeated them over again
to your lover, your children, your spouse,
you suspect one day you'll be repeating
to the bored nurse changing your drip
or checking your catheter. A run
on face masks, so that the subway begins
to resemble the Tokyo underground.
The Masque of the Red Death played out
under the palms, around the swimming pool.
        Left standing how many reft
        of anger's conduit gender's misaligned

enthusiasm it must be the
system always the system ossified
malice privilege they're counting heads

and bodies marking down movements
tracking vital spreads viral diffusions
information false illness real perfect
shared germs bestowed and shared
factoids fading chill the crisp

morning light of late winter
snowdrops and crocuses strewn across
the straw-brown grass the blunt
nuzzling force of folded blind
tulips pushing their way up

from under mulch and leaves
carapaces of wool and leather
gradually shed the lawn alive
with squirrels the air shimmering
with early birdsong this early

March morning year Twenty Twenty
of the Common Era so-called
still worried about *Original Sin*
so-called the *crooked timber* thing
the bent that bends us

from what would do us
best *intelligence* by no means
a *moral category* but *attention*
with a stronger claim surely
than anything else I know

the *Fall* into homily sermon
when rite has become perfunctory
maybe the Papists had it
right all incense and droning
foreign tongues majestic music robes

every sort of enrapturement save
the rhetorical and *see here*
refighting the Reformation a half-
millennium late as if the
sky hadn't emptied itself clean

before your father's mother's birth
before Europe twice unleashed its
abattoirs across the continents before
topping your neighbor's genocide became
the sport of grubby people's

tribunes. They canceled History
prematurely, at least a season or two
early. *What hurts*. All of us blinded

Cyclopes yammering our tormentors' names
and blaming no one in particular.

The winter was gentle, mild, this time
around. Spring springs up as usual,

eternal, though we've confused the poppies
with over-eager cherry blooms.

64.

It was about the beginning
of September, 1664, that I,
among the rest of my neighbours,
heard, in ordinary discourse,
that the plague was returned again
in Holland; for it had been
very violent there, and particularly
at Amsterdam and Rotterdam,
in the year 1663— It mattered not
from whence it came; but all agreed
it was come into Holland again.
"It broke our little ballerina's heart
when they canceled the dance company
concert, and all her hours at the barre,
before the mirror, were for nothing."
Under the new-old banner *No Man*
An Island, they're suspending all gatherings
for the foreseeable future, shuttering
the shops, setting an invisible picket
around every outlander—until it's blown
over, when we'll come together in conclave
under the blades of our trusty Switzers
and send up the curl of white smoke
that signals a new, reformed Pope.

The magnolia, having held its breath
the better part of a week, has exploded

into pink frothy blossom. Forsythia snarls
in every direction, and daffodils bow

their heads bare to the still chilly
wind. I hear the rhythmic, then aperiodic

slap of a basketball across the street,
trust the cars buzzing by—so few—

bear their passengers on necessary
errands. All over the world, poets

are writing verses about isolation,
novelists plotting pandemic fictions.

The girl is in her room now—the trains
running only on a skeleton schedule—

listening with one ear to the oracle
of her laptop. One boy is down the shore,

another just over the hill, though it might
as well be across the continent.

She is traversed and torn apart
by fears and passions: she wants,

and yearns to be wanted. Her eyesight,
her hearing, are mediated through screens

speakers and invisible waves. Sometimes
she wonders if she isn't herself a machine.

The boy down the shore plays at black-
clad Hamlet, who called his own body

this machine. The dye was a failure, only made
her hair darker. The world is a prison.

The oldest stories told how the Elves awoke
under a canopy of stars before the sun

and moon were manufactured. The physics
of it all is fabulous, laughable, and came

to give its Redactor second thoughts. One author—
"Priestly" so-called—wrote a creation account,

and another—the "Jahwist"—wrote a second,
only roughly similar. And their Redactor

felt no need to harmonize or combine
the two stories, just set them side by side

in sublime contradiction. We lie to others
so often that the untruths gradually, easily,

displace what was in our memory. Someone
should have said that. His aphorisms, the Obituarist

wrote, were well-turned but shopworn.
The best passages of his productions—both

prose and verse—turn out to be, on closer
examination, half-remembered echoes

of others' letters. The machine breaks down
over time; the Second Law of Thermodynamics

is more, after all, than suggested
best practices. The Founding Fathers are speaking

to us on a videotape—VHS, Betamax—found
somewhere in the archive of the dead city.

Some of them are grim and determined, bags
clearly visible under their eyes. (At that stage

of the plague, the bacillus was widely rumored
to lurk in the cosmetic pots of the TV

makeup crews.) Others are fresh from the tanning bed,
shirts and lapels pressed crisp, ad-libbing

with remarkable aplomb from prepared scripts,
radiating empathy, reassurance. They seem

pathetically quaint, the parish-by-parish statistics,
the bills of mortality nailed up each day around

the church doors. The Founding Fathers say, *Don't*
worry too much. This too, they say, *shall pass.*

The Founding Fathers quote T. S. Eliot, they quote
Ecclesiastes, they fumble their blurred memories

of the Apostle's great panegyric on Charity, bring
out all their sounding brasses and tinkling cymbals.

The magnolia butts against a pewter sky, its upper
blossoms fully, deliriously open. Its lower twigs

and branches are sprinkled with pink ovoids,
on the verge of explosion. They shift and rustle

in the wind, shiver against the cold, steady
rain, the thumb-large flakes of late snow.

65.

Who would spill into the seamless night, heave
the abductor apart? With what conjuration
do you address yourself to the exploit,
the token bypass? Clogged larvae, coagulate
gelid astonishment, were all they could descry
from the cabin, that abscessed and malodorous
primal scene. They joined us there, together we re-
arranged and shuffled densely printed blanks.

About logic they were rarely wrong, those old
        masters, their outlandish clothes
and gorgeous hairdos. Their elaborate ruffs
        and buttery, finely-tooled leather shoes.
Buckles, tassels, silver-headed walking
        sticks. Goose quills and microscopes,
spyglasses and nodding plumes. A camouflage
        bikini, a silk and latex trousseau.
The oracles and sages strut their way
        up the catwalk, toss their heads
at the turn. Syllogism and stemmata,
        quicksilver delta of the calculus
and hungry glimmer of philosopher's stone.
        Names are sequent to things named, said
        someone: *consequentia rerum*, but requisite
        for any useful grasp of phenomena.
        Kaleidoscope of the world sliced
        into graspable gobbets, shapes
        modes attributes and other Latin words.
        The teacher says, *Salve, discipuli*; when

the virtual session ends, *vale*. The teacher
says, *fermez vos livres*. You're trying
to make sense of a new world by reading
old books again, week in which each day
has lost its surname, so _____day follows ____day,
followed by undifferentiated ____day.
Me, I'm always waiting, that's what I do.
Lamp trimmed and ready, *parousia*-gear stashed
in a handy cupboard. My Aunt Anne
would be in her element, downstairs closet
filled top to bottom with discount
toilet rolls. The rain almost gentle today.
A block off someone hammers something.

Tangled in the stirrups, we were dragged and chastened
under the roar of clouds. Socially, nominally,
scene shifting like the blown calendar leaves
in another millennium's movie.
Bewildered accelerationism's avatar thumb-
twirling sinks into screens. Full-on Spring—
no denying, who could spill into the seamless
night? When the Revelator died, the hardscrabble
sect—several thousands by then—expected
something to happen: they had been expecting so long,
trimmed and ready, waiting for Bad
to go Worse and turn some corner or other.
We had Joy Division on the system
when we remembered to turn it on: "She's
Lost Control," "Day of the Lords,"

"Isolation," had New Order cued up
for a synth-pop party at the first decent
opportunity. Full-bore, full-blown, racket
of birdsong and canine chantry. Lithe
and playful squirrels, occasional foxes
bold in the streets. Third Avenue, Park,
alight and echoing. The sun filters through
after a grey morning, windy tumultuous
night. Seamless night, seamless days,
tense to the point of ragged.

66.

The truly wise measure their options,
weigh advantage and expediency,
and always bow to necessity, necessity being
after all what it is. The wise
do not scramble syntax or confuse
effect for cause—admit causality
if not as inevitability, then as good
as inevitable. The wise know the world
is the manifestation of *God or Nature,*
know the world is a synchronous virtual
reality placed in their mind by God, know
the world is flickering shadows cast
by firelight, resembling in vague outline
actual creatures walking in a sun
the wise can only imagine.

        The polite young attendant, Muslim, a heavy
beard pressing under his surgical mask, told us the rabbi
        and limousine had just left. We had missed
the funeral by five minutes. Maimed rites. Acres
        of empty parking lots. Park closed, but off
among a glade of vigorously budding trees a knot
        of kids are playing with fire. A coil
of blue smoke, blurring the trunks beyond.
                Flashes, intermittencies: a morning
                and afternoon of driving rain and cutting
                winds; then, toward dusk, the sky clears,
                the sun flashes through—and
                the backyard's unearthly radiant green.

It took my breath away to see it.
Today or yesterday, they said,
and it would all begin
to wind down. Bear
or bull market in tears, lives.
Quicksilver progression
from arithmetic to geometrical.
The wise have clear and distinct
ideas how it all fits: the coil
of blue smoke, the apologetic
youth closing fast the chain-link
gate with rubber-gloved hands.

They're running only two ferries a day. We were
on the last, Long Island—or was it the banks
of the James?—had drifted out of sight
hours ago. No dream: we had wheeled
the amps and a skeletal drum kit
into the cargo bay, paid the supplementals,
kept our guitars with us snug in padded
gig bags. We were playing the Kismet Inn,
maybe the Casbah, the Hotel Xanadu, Hotel
Zion. There would be fried fish, beer.
There would be men in t-shirts and sandals
talking earnestly to women half their age.
Hotel Caledonia on the farther shore, under
the wink of the lighthouse, turning and shining
and growing no closer. We bobbed up

and down only, the gulls in the dusk
passed us by, laughing.

Good Friday to Easter
Sunday static blank unrecorded
day silence stunned apostles
Mary Salome James etc

    denial unrecognition redhaired Iscariot
    pieces of repentant silver
    stunned silence brittle trimmed
    and reader unrecognizing unprophetic

        the next thing next
        day what happens now
        when will something happen
        powerless to be born

    prophecy said the Blessed
    not foreknowledge but imagination
    rhetoric not science persuasion
    cut and tailored for

an audience projections dates
epistemic curves models cellular
tracking fear and anxiety
fear of stark death

A free man thinks of nothing less than death,
said someone. Said easily. One word follows
another. *His meditation is a meditation, not on death,*
but on life. It makes an aphorism.

67.

That thing you forgot to do last year
has turned out to be important. The little noise
under the hood that irritated you so much
at first, until you got to where you ignored it,
has turned out to be a symptom of something big,
expensive. That mole on your back. Catch in your throat.
Bill you accidentally threw away, bank statement
you misplaced. I found your phone number,
I'm embarrassed to say, stuck as a bookmark
between pages 42 and 43 of a book
I gave up reading four years ago. I'm texting
you now. There's a clown show on TV
every afternoon, a remote read-through of *'Tis Pity*
She's a Whore. All my friends are sharing
pictures of their children, their meals.
Someone says invisible rays are stoking
the plague. Someone else tells me the windmills
are feeding my tumors. In the grocery, the separation
between organic and GMO is as rigidly enforced
as that between kosher and treyf, and with as much
logic. If I had a clear and distinct idea
of where I was going, I'd know what to do next.
Maybe listen to a record, pour a glass of some
exotic but cheap liqueur, light a fat spliff.
The first one—ah, the tragedy!—rolled over
Nick's feet, that warm evening last spring, fell
between the boards into the water below. The second
hit me hard, knocked me off my feet

like I hadn't been knocked before. We're all
older than we've ever been—wry cliché. Younger, also,
than we'll be tomorrow morning. Our Savior, scripture
says, went forty days without food or society,
and afterwards was *hungry*. Fast then temptation

Citing scripture to th'accuser's face
temple pinnacle kingdoms of earth
sons of pride to be compared
state of war exemption nasty
brutish a scramble among crumbs

Abraham's bosom Lazarus in glory
Dives proper name or class
designator formations of production determining
consciousness shepherds oxen and particolored
kine huddled in apartments tenanted

Overborne edgeworth and outwearied for
Jesus' sweet sake implore thee
open the tomb stratum by
stratum and dating our discontent
by the styles of potsherds

Autumn Gold Avocado of childhood
toothpaste cars of pre-millennial angst
diggings flocked embroidered and hemmed
with Mallarmé's abolished lacework gracefully
turned fleeced faun's thigh stooped

For the golden apples t'ignore
the ravening board bright red
flesh sexually differentiated by skin
tone though streaming identical coiffures
signal *Idomeneus* or just *archer*
and these our bones ought be found
in the fourth stratum, just below
the second great burning
that melted all the glass and circuit
boards into Pollock dribbles
of color veining the soil
red clay and yellow sedimentary
rocks, hauled out in paper bag after bag
each successive one minding me
of the dead cat I dug up with
my friends at eight or nine, the squirrel
I tipped with a shovel-end into a new
hole behind the garage—
by five minutes, missed the funeral
and in the fourth stratum, where the living
walked in concentric circles, dancing-floor
of a grand Troy-town saloon, the soft
green leathers of Oz and the Castro
Gypsum blocks softened by rain
shattered frescos rebuild themselves into
blueprints three strata down for
concrete and rebar pillars astonishingly
anticipate Art Deco Miami Beach

Under the sun the bruising
rain set to competition diggers
both Turk and Hellene selfsame
taskmaster hornéd English Pharaoh hawk's
profile but frontal kohl-rimmed eye

Drop of water great fixéd
gulf stratum and stratum means
of production earth groans beneath
history weight of misery heavens
opening just another technicolor vista

The first rainbow was miraculous
only because first their diggings
find stratum under stratum until
shovel-tips scrape boneless rock soft
dull fur of the wee

Thing paws clasped as if
in petition ground under our
soles a compost of dying
petitioners cards papers and soft
tissue melting into yellow sediment

68.

The Peacock Room, and the Thalia:
plush seats of the Grand Odeon,
packed and hushed for opening night,
the premiere: we arrived by limousine,
by commandeered SUVs and bespoke
Italian sportscars: our eyes pulsed
and ached briefly through the gauntlet
of flashing cameras: the Grand Opening—
unctuous paragraphs from The Chair,
then a newsreel: yet again, The Fall
of the Dictators, the statues hoicked down,
ticker-tape parades: plague's end,
Reconstruction, the laying of cornerstones
and cutting of ribbons: planting
of ceremonial trees:

And that in abeyance the day Edmund,
Peter, Lucy, and Susan unearthing
from litter of potsherds and cinders
the cold amphorae of wan days.
BLEACH said their graphemes,
SUNLIGHT and VITAMIN D. Light
on the beach sand wetted grey,
scurry clouds and leadless doggos,
good boys without exception.

Peter and Edmund grinning to display
pectorals tanned and waxed hairless
oiled armpits, cock-rings and appliances

sundry on display. The breeze did lift
the little golf-course flags, and lifted
their stout engines were. Joiner and pipe-
fitter, a-stroll on nubbly beach, sand to polish
and shine the planes of their arrogance,
smooth away razor-burn and stubble.

Susan would cry she her little bird-
cries, nether lips asquirm in the bite
of Lucy's teeth, but Edmund heaving
trajectory across the table of Lucy's back
ought make mock of brother's mischance,
coils of early eggwhite release dabbling
Susan's axillary fur. Amphorae guarded
disinterred sunlight, coiled and spiraled
clouds mock foreshadow their knotted forms.

Tally-ho, said Susan, bit between teeth,
rowels buried in Peter's ribby sides. Amphorae
yawn, glisten, depths shimmer of oil
and bleach and hygienic lubricants.
Tally-ho, sang the oven-bird, and *pieces
of eight*. As the ship's-cook lean crutched
himself across the sand. As Edmund writhed
under expert ministrations, the sun's or wind's
or other doughty forms of *Natura naturans*.

Will growl and jostle, amphorae, handles pricked
picked out with nymphal satyric scenes.

Topography models a landskip dried and
spent. Susan's black tresses wound round
white and opulent neck, fair down
and freckles across shoulders. Print
of two sets of teeth orbit Edmund's
left nipple. Slurry of sister's dorsal
skin beneath Peter's disgraceful nails.

Thieves in the jars, amphorae cameras.
To cut action splice and hot up generally
beneath windy sun, fulgent argent day.
Hasty riddance of damp bathing gear,
castaway into scenic surf. Lubricious
damp and laboring damp dried in fulgent
windy sun. Under the mass reflectors, angles
of light to dance across ribby sides
nubbly pack'd strained and banded abdomens.

        Last rays of the sun splintered on the mostly calm
waters, Antonio would brush the sand from his salt-
        stiffened trunks, Antonietta would pluck idly
at an asp of seaweed coiled across her thigh.
        The cocktails have gone warm, or been drunk,
the last Italian ices have melted into the dunes.
        Tony and Toni came for the Mermaid Parade,
stayed for the salt, oil, and spray. Will find
        their way back, with all the other weary
subway riders, in the gathering dusk.

69.

They set us to digging, to plant things they said,
	but there were no flowers or shrubs in sight.
We weren't to be our own grave-diggers, evidently—
	at command, we shoveled slow and careful.
The first inches under the leaves and yellow grass
	were rich dark humus, full of worms.
Soon our spades clinked on potsherds,
	which we lifted gently, brushed clean.
Sandy unearthed a six-inch steatopygian fetish,
	which set Sir Arthur's eyes alight.
Breathless, he used the long nail of his fourth
	finger to trowel the dirt from between
her formidable buttocks, from under her monumental
	breasts. The Professor was less excited:
it would not do, she said, to waste their attention
	on relics of praehistoric lubriciousness, however
gracefully carved their ivory curves, now a rich
	tobacco brown with time. Beneath the potsherds
was a layer of mingled plaster and ash,
	veined with the charcoal of burned beams.
The sack of the city!, said Sir Arthur, eyes
	alight, well-thumbed broken-spined copies
of the canonical epics peeping from the pockets
	of his tweeds. Underneath that was what had clearly
been a server room: air-conditioning ductwork, metal shelving,
	hectare upon hectare of corroded microchips
and countless leagues of brittle cabling. The sun was low
	in the sky on the third day of the dig

when we shoveled aside the last of that rubble,
        and broke through into the chamber of the amphorae.

Sans joy sans feeling sans
        all concomitant boatload of rising
        affect heart surges, mapping aperiodic
        cameral voices or extramural barometric
        shifts. Did they obey immediately,
        did they revolve spontaneously their
        phantasmal grievances, privilege lost reacquired
        in imagination's demesne? Where could
such exigencies end, at what point

Would the traceries of twilight
        lisping pedantic assume a more
        serious tone, even take hold
        of the Foucauldian labyrinth—knowledge,
        power, the whole familiar jingle—
        embedded in their city's doorsills?
        Open elate their fiery portals,
        regard insinuate the closed and
squeamish valetudinarian days, the uncovered pit.

Drunkenness and chambering, she scorned,
        menu paschal and pentecostal. Tongues
        of doves and fire, blazing
        Hebrew particles, the engraved tablets
        raptured in intermittent moments. Glossalalia
        spectrum off the charts, remixed

        unconstantly for deep house sleepy
        dance party rave, or simple
gentle relinquishment of primary motor control.

Starstruck spelunker, to take wholly
        in that petal-fallen landscape, homestead
        terrifically pressed ironed and flocked
        by floral nebulae, cherry blossoms
        passing time with laconic descent.
        Hacked and fitted, ambient slurred
        to a rising forenoon before
        an early afternoon imperiled sleep.
A dog's life, cat's life, lethargic alertness

Dragged from arbitrary to indifferent,
        and what are you doing
        today? Seven weeks that one
        embellishment to promise renewed novelty
        homogeneity disappointed, sun risen bravely
        on same old same old,
        l'avenir and *futur* juggle between
        hands and pages smeared with
sundry impacted economies, nightcaps well rotated.

        Drink to me only infant
        mole infant joy curled
        in expiring warmth across
        the front lawn's grass

The birds summon their great
parliament of winds last year's
leaves shored in heaps
against the basement door

My calves' whiteness shows
the length of winter passed
constellation of dandelion
seeds powdering the grass

In the corner of my eye
the chipmunk flickers
across a red cushion
on a weathered wood

Settee trees aflame
with young leaves old
mole newborn year soft
pliant and still warm

70. *Disconnected Remarks*

For the most part tranquil the night
the moon tangled in branches
a dead or deathly glow to the east
                    Flame to ashes hours gone, neighbor's
tiki torch snuffed and a single car.
From humble to humiliated
part of the general contract,
rarely ground down but always
available to that mercy. Grandees
                    and burgermeisters, hoarders
of capital imaginary and real,
cycling through lunar phases, to recess
                    and happily recover.
Too much pressure and the innertube
ruptures awkwardly sometimes. You don't
expect at the best of times,
                    petal-flecked rain grating
                    and the sated rats
of the underworld. The London underground
almost defeated them, black smudges
                    of the rubber buffers across
my mother's temples. She wiped them off
with a saliva-moistened Kleenex.
                    Two-year-separated dyad,
                    she and her sister—in that
like her granddaughters. And her friend
in that chill moment at the funeral home—
did she mean to sear and shame me?
Meaning or not, she did. Some things

                        you never live past, forget.
                        Some excavations go too deep,
the amphorae quarter-filled with slime
of wine—or outright poison. The Canadian
Premier, seeing Sir Arthur's fanciful reconstructions,
                        remarked how strikingly they anticipated
Art Deco: "When did you say," he winked, "they were made?"
Across a martini glass, the clear blue eyes
of a remarkable Waterhouse "stunner."
                        How often do we meet, she said,
someone who sees us as we long to be seen?
My mother loved me with a fierce timid
and baffled love. Mine was the worst
                        betrayal, bar none. How antique
                        in the unforgiving morning light,
how quaint and changed. For *dignified by age*
read *lacerated by remorse*. For *achieving*
a remarkable voice read *with a knack*
for intermittently successful ventriloquy.

I have her book, the poems she typed
            and had bound—*Heart Songs*.
Decades of letters and diaries,
            a weekly round, a seasonal
round, in a hand that varied
            only with the pen it held.

She was guileless when voicing
            her love—never casually—

or her scorn—more rarely still.
   Her virtues were humility
and patience, good will and hope
   in an unseen reward.

I grew beyond her expectations
   into something alien, familiar
yet disproportioned. Aging, her incongruously
   predatory nose juts from my shapeless
mug. Did I disappoint her? Who
   knows. I disappoint myself.

A lifting at times, almost, of the weight
of everything and nothing, the seams and grainy
textures of each surface, strange residues
that resist the scrubbing cloth, neurotic
ideologemes stuck in the mind's corners,
car horns at the traffic light. Lifts and pauses,
like the clouds yesterday towards sunset,
so the almost level sunbeams fell smack
on the azaleas down the street, transfiguring
them into Pixar magenta flame. Or when
the bass slides in under a patter of percussion,
distant ululating, a wash of almost-
cheesy synths, enters along with Gigi's voice,
straining from Abyssinia to Zion—reaching
it—buoyed by those busy, warm clouds.

71.

Sunday morning's business, essential
we were told. We're still waiting
to be saved, after all. *Heilsgeschichte*
on the syllabus, at the next
exit, around the bent unseen.
Early spring passes its sell-by
date, the rhododendron cut down
and thrown on the winnowing heap.
The world-spirit evolving sorts lists
and consigns us. Sunday morning
rises with hope or apathy
in its train. We dropped by
the conclave, but the conclave was shuttered,
found a new gate across the entrance
to the friendly catacombs, cozy dojo
of clavicle-and-femur bookcases.
All that was solid seemed to be melting
into broadband and remote access.
We heard stories about the starving rats,
dolphins in the canals, new colonies
of moles around the neglected foundations.
I tried to tell you jokes, you tried
to time your laughlets to the digital lag.

Cat-calls and huzzahs purple-black fringing
their daybreak mounted communication break
and a low scrape cherrypicker
power lines wrapped in branches
baize gives way to meadow

Stalled on the tarmac reticulated
and filtered bus broken down
no gas on the freeway
why continue anyone wonders
if it no longer *sparks joy*

Inevitably surprising steals catlike behind
and changes willy-nilly your life
mage on the doorstep closet
full of musty out-of-fashion sashes
staple of some erotic sub-genre

Sub-genre of interruption of ruined
edgy or *edging* discourses trembling
suspicious *sub rosa* spilling *red-black*
simultaneous sanguine and melancholic Ashkenaz
the blurt among the babble

Shutting abruptly down the feed
wavy compressed cable short undetectable
to the naked eye practiced
polished the *sound* conceals itself
in the player's practiced touch

Silent the cat-calls and wolf-
        whistles, silent the applause; that
                was the time of living-room

concerts, muffed beginnings and dodgy
camera angles, the triumphant return
of the *tableau vivant,* young women
massing their hair, rolling themselves
in curtains and towels, sprawled
languid Rossetti or Schiele—ironical
but anxious, as the Angel
of Sidelong Irony surrendered her throne
to the Angel of Fretful Angst.
April arrived, the sun came
back, and we were
not saved.

What, discipuli, does the rain do?
The rain *pours,* it *rushes,* it *descends.*
Grass, shrubs, needles and leaves, washed
and laved. *Total immersion,* even.
The grass will blot out the chalk horses.
The grass will engulf our feet and the heads
of our carved stones.

72. *Septuagint | Jubilees*

for Tyrone Williams

It was a starting gate, it was Black
    Friday at Walmart or Costco,
it was The Who in Cincinnati, 1979
    (long before you were born, you tell
the child). But no it was nothing
    at all like that—nothing at all.
It was four hundred years in the boiler
    room, it was the sound of men
working on the chain gang, it was "Preaching
    the Blues" and "Crossroads"
and jagged dub "Exodus" all at once.
    It was "Redemption Song," but electric.
When the barriers fell the crowd washed
    forward they were throwing water
and alcohol their heads were on fire
    buildings melting with water
or flames all the colors washing
    from the pavement needles rising
on the potentiometers unprecedented
    happening yet again taking
stock taking place words usually
    blown billowed losing
color and contour got harder-edged
    crystallized in the air before
our eyes space behind the visors
    and mirror shades reflecting us
black for once not beaten blue
    so that running the streets

strangely carless ankle-deep in colored
        fluids market backwash the voices
ricocheted from one plywood storefront
        across to another without dissolving
into sludge coalesced in consensual
        astonishment into parousial
soteriological crystal the words
        in all their faceted variations

A tatter of squirrel's tail, forgotten
on the back lawn; auto noise,
        by degrees returning, now back
        to full volume; how did I get
here? masked and distanced,
a curious bubble away
        from Babylon and its torments;
        the ranging song of street-
birds and scrubbing machines,
four-octave descent of the tired
        and jubilantly drunk night
        porter.
When she raised her arms to adjust
her ponytail, the hairs
        of her armpits glistened briefly
        in the late afternoon sun.
I felt my breath quicken.
That hank of tail, now
        draped across the wire mesh
        of the little firepit, too warm

to roast marshmallows. Silver
guard-hairs moving
        in the wind, swaying
        with the auto noise.

Ho gegrapha, gegrapha—or was it *quod*
scripsi scripsi? Native outlander tongue:
fundamental, and inerrant. To be read
literally, for the plain sense. Plain, plane,
flat, horizontal. The lowest stratum,
bedrock. It begins with division, ends
with a curse. Or reconciliation, depending.

The Founding Fathers, unsure handlers
of the traders' *lingua franca,* calqued
the rapid interplay of baffled wonder
and dazzling allusion onto merchants'
hard currency, explained obtusely
the puns and twists of sound. Panic
birdsong, transposed for the kazoo.

They took *their* text from the Convocation
of Seventy-Two, whose miraculous separate
consensus struck the divine words
into identical Greek in only twelve times
the duration the Lord occupied himself making
the world. Barter an *alpha* for an *alef,*
omega for an end to labor, jubilee.

Split reed or feather quill, they drew—
not pressed—the breath across the page,
unfamiliar left to right notating the flicker
of tongues of fire, pigeons' wings, mouthing
the hard *gammas* and abrupt *chis*, screwing
their eyes and fingers tight against
inevitable eyeskip and blot.

Fifty years, a century, half a millennium—
an end to all this bartering, this
translation, spidery Gothic and streamlined
Gill mapped, calqued, palimpsested
over the flickering tongues: Serious
and bearded, in ruffs turbans and burnooses,
seventy and two: *quod scripsi scripsi.*

> The inscriptions grew cruder with each successive
> stratum, the letters more ill-formed, punctuation
> mostly absent. If we dug further, we sensed,
> the stones would say something altogether
> different from the received text. We were happy,
> then, to find the last layer forbidden.
> They made us lay aside our shovels and trowels,
> shuffle off for a break. The curves, once so graceful,
> had disappeared, replaced by jagged angles, angular
> corners: easier by far to carve in hard-yielding
> stone. They came before us, but they *were* us.
> We spoke suddenly in their voices, each in her
> or his own tongue they heard us—there were doves

descending, and tongues of flame—it was like
a camp meeting under canvas, almost—
and we preached a new song, old
song's variation, whose words felt
blocky and strange, longer in the short
bits and vice-versa, everybody in their own
language and idiom, echoes ricocheting
off the older echoes, the plywood, the broken
glass now flowing crystal water. They wouldn't tell us,
didn't want us to know, but we divined it anyway—
under that last stratum, grim-faced angular
clay tablets, was the water—not just
the water, the beach itself, salt and gritty
and blown with a clear piscine air.

73.

We resisted the voices from the intercom
when we could understand
what they were saying.
Social media archaeologists
issued detailed suggestions
on how best to topple
—safely, efficiently—
the most hateful obelisks.
The country was littered—
the public squares, playgrounds,
the railway station concourses—
with old men from a century
or more ago, medusa'd
into stone, wincing or frowning
their triumphs and benevolence.
They leaned forward, were arrested
in their falling only by the inevitable
earth. A moment's silence we
prayed, stoppage to the endless
noise, rancor, contumely, the cracking
of the whips and yelps
of interrupted innocence: the girl
practicing a four-octave scale,
the movements of a pas-de-deux;
writing a poem or singing a brief,
unmodulating melody. Her friendships
are strung out across tenuous
bandwaves and screens; her shoes,

stinking of chemical novelty, have
        bubble-wrapped and vacuum-packed
themselves from somewhere in China.
The rattle of wagons on the boardwalk,
        eyes passing over masks
and bandanas, mourning doves and patient
laboring surf—vivid trivia, wrappers
        circling in a tide-pool, as the ocean
draws a deep breath, steps back
to pounce and wash us all loose.

The first commandment was division,
to raise levees and sea-walls, hedgerows
and CCTV. Then they commanded us
to stay home, to forsake the civic rites
and festal days, abandon the gilded
pantheon and huddle with the *lares penatesque.*

Better the sun on the sand, glittering strip-
mall, or the morbidly hushed streets?
Blunt busy signal or endlessly unfolding
hold music? Our alternatives—for the lucky ones
who had them—were fixed, unfixed, impossible
to count. Accounts of symptoms changed

daily: our eldest read them off to us
from news feeds, from random chat rooms,
from what used to be "word of mouth."
The third and fourth commandments, reversing

their precursors, then themselves, followed
swiftly. In abrupt succession a whole

decalogue or more—we lost count.
Who could flourish in these data-rich
hothouses? The percussionists' idle rest
through the whole third movement; loaf's
second rise, eagerly awaited but taking
its own sweet time. *Strange patches*

on the skin, alarmingly varicolored; luster
falling from the hair; looseness of the teeth,
discoloration; heightened sensitivity
in the extremities (both physical and existential);
disturbances in the visual field—contraction
of the periphery, asymmetrical blind spots;

shortness of breath, or oversaturation of oxygen
through all the tiny, most tender capillaries;
shields of new bone distorting the forehead;
withering of limbs, unaccountable changes
in vocal timbre. So Susan or Peter recounted,
depending on who was eldest that day,

though for all we knew the blobby voice
from the ceiling might be saying
the same thing, or something like.
Directives counter-directives diktats

and recommendations. Slurries of doubtful
omens, telenovellas and sagas of misdirection.

We held tight to the children, we crouched
apart, shivered in reluctant springtime.
We shouted the mantras of normality,
forgetting that "normal" was only the number
of a previous beast—gross Behemoth, shining
Leviathan, unhappy, shambling Minotaur.

Flesh famished for want
of touch, shrinking back
into itself. Whorled pads
of fingertips, concavities
of palm, the dark and secret
hollow at the inside
of the thigh. Another's limbs
moving out of rhythm,
then echoing your own systole
and diastole.

To lay in, around a bird-cage
of bone, the sinuous
tubing and combed flesh,
the skin patterned with freckles,
stretched taut, folded in minute
pleats—my palm to your shoulder,
the fivefold constancy
of your fingers against my hip-

bone—the tight-packed flesh,
giving way to soft pressure,
contracting itself startled and hard
beneath twofold hands.
The space between charged with meaning,
anticipation, prickly
and short-breathed at the shapes
and contingencies of desperate
and deferred contact.

The spirit is willing, always, whether
pneuma or *psyche*; the meat
machines are always breaking down.
Band-aids, splints, Ace bandages
salves ointments and unguents
accumulate and pass their sell-by
dates. Drones deliver them; the shark-like
ambulance is electric and driverless.
We are laid out spread-eagled
and trembling under lights, examined
probed and catalogued onto screens,
touched by hands not at all.

74.

Warrant error. Incompatible warrants. Turtles
all the way down. Solid rock, shifting sands.
Wise man built his house. Priest all shaven
and shorn. Choir-stall empty, angelic, bare
ruined—who could hear me crying out?

Without stain. Unmarked by claws, emotional
scratching-post. Crush, orange or other-
wise. In both senses Mosaic. My assembly
built upon this rock, this stony ground.
The ground of faith, in Luther's geography,

beneath the left nipple. Salvation by faith
alone seized him squatting in the privy,
hard and recalcitrant stool. Fundamentalism.
Inclining of the spirit, or bowels of mercy.
An affair of the body, a lust for origins.

Every idol a graven image—written
in his little book, not exactly tautological
but so near as to make little
difference. Parse out the distinction, will you,
between rites and solemnities of worship

and obsession ineluctably turned attention.
Something to do with sociality, maybe,
the warmth of bodies pressed together
in uncomfortable pews. Parasitic
and tenuous childhood, conclaved

in government-issue living rooms, auditoriums
furnished with unfamiliar, heterodox hymnals,
strangely angled pulpits, padded kneelers—
an altar-screen hinting at forbidden
and garish representation—*graven images.*

A book, as always, was behind it all—
scroll or codex or bundle of mimeo'd
pages, spiral-bound. Author unknown,
subject of scores of lifetimes
huddled in museums, monasteries, libraries,

eyes reading themselves blind by candle-
or fluorescent light. The light refracted
through the lawn's green spears,
it seemed that day, refuted
all claims of origin: that butterfly

the only authority, and not to be
consulted or obeyed. Blue-black
butterfly the only *psyche,* spirit; afternoon
breeze—blessedly dry—the only *pneuma*
to be felt. Enfleshed—under the left nipple.

The bus passed suburban neighborhoods,
shrubbery and trees and flags, the industrial
marshes, warehouses and refineries looming
up from tracts of wetland. Muscovy ducks
turned their beaks quizzically as we passed,

the ramparts and towers, steel and glass,
glowering across the river before us:
ziggurats, hanging gardens, stepped pyramids:
passed into the tunnel, endless and antiseptic—
lit by day and night, dry and dripping—

And when we finally emerge, we wondered,
will the theater district still be there?
Opening night to empty seats. The Kenosis
Revue, Parousia Follies. Yes, it's been a strange
and wobbly summer, after a bitter and lonely

spring. Harvest almost upon us, and still no hint
of salvation. Salvation part of the warrant,
imcompatible, illusory. The last-act intervention,
quasi-messianic promise. False prophets,
graven images, gospel in broken fonts.

The scriptorium was a-hum when we arrived,
our tour guide a bright-faced young man
with a fashy haircut, black-rimmed glasses,
and a tie bar. A thousand nibs scratching
at once, a thousand authoritative copies

crawling out, line by line, before our eyes.
It was a Printing House in Hell, it was
the Algonquin Round Table, it was Boswell
taking notes on a napkin, it was Plato
dictating to Socrates, it was John the Divine

pulling back the curtain on Oz the Great
and Powerful—a thousand nibs scratching,
and the Word made Flesh before our eyes,
line by line, like snowflakes no two
copies alike. The Word fruiting

and multiplying. Someone said Truth
was one and single, and someone else
said Truth was single and three,
and someone at the back of the tour
started scribbling down stemmata—

They printed the wrong draft, I murmured.
Mosaic in all senses, you said, blue
eyes crinkling with a hint of a smile—
in the gloom, the gold gathers
the light—Byzantium or Zion,

the emerald spectacles of Oz,
sunlight dappled across the back lawn.
The green world a scrim of renewal
on the proliferating, originless myriads
of mirror-fragments, shell-casings, rolling-

papers, curling-papers, baking-parchment,
mummy-wrappers. Bakhtin used his own
manuscript—on realism—to roll cigarettes;
up in smoke, as well, Carlyle's first *French*
Revolution, thanks to John Stuart Mill's

chamber-maid. A compact continuous scroll,
the *120 Days,* added to daily in crabbed,
miniscule cursive, screwed into a tight
cyclinder and shoved into a crevice in the cell
wall. A gospel indeed, with ten variations

for each of its apostles, each of the twelve
tribes. *You're counting things again,* you
murmured, gently nudging me. *But there are,*
I gasped, *more variations among witnesses*
than words in the whole testament—error,

vagrancy, wandering—a gospel of variations,
seventy-two or 120 or however many days
they rode that bus back and forth around
the desert, the forty years. No single
DeMille moment at Oreb or Sinai,

no Ten or Three or even One. The sunlight
on the lawn is one, but the green—
and the red, and the black—are a shifting
mosaic—in all senses. An error, wandering,
in the warrant. All the way down, and beyond.

75.

The *Sheltered Night*; or,
the *Shuttered Night*.
Evening air heavy
with moisture, at its edge
a chill that might
be fall. The steps
of the museum are empty
now, sidewalks—crowded
six months ago—mostly
deserted. Insect sounds
echo across the river,
among the buildings.
We stumble and cough,
warily—touch our phones
and order in, tip
the delivery-person
at a distance. Across
the rooms of sixth-floor
apartments, old friends
are cautiously toasting
one another, hoping
for something more. We hold
our breath on the subway,
watch the meter, count
the statistics. The voices
on our phones say *family*,
say *compassion*, say
decent. A man handles
a stringed instrument

on the screen, fiddles
with the tuning keys, slides
a capo to the comfortable
fret. First time around
this was magical, a step
into the inner sanctum,
a *glimpse of paradise*
across a dull and bitter land.
Faëry from down the street,
across town—now it's stale,
flat, uncomfortable. Empire
state of tedium, empire
of heightened senses, high
tension, worry. Empire
of Anxiety. Maybe
we took on too much,
tried to do too many things
at once. The day
is dry, warm. A helicopter thrums
overhead, a truck roars out
below. Shirt-cuff notes, in
the moment. Each pair
of pedestrians seems to wear
matching shoes. That pigeon sitting
on the lamppost for what seems
like hours. Impromptu parade
of cyclists, blocks long—weaving,
popping wheelies, hanging onto cars—
celebrating nothing but the motionless

heat of the day and their own
movement. What better
to celebrate, rejoice, than
the irreducible motion?

76.

The child an animal to be tamed,
made human, softened and planed, fitted
in the missing puzzle-piece space,
fine gradations and subtly lived conditions,
a green light to walk. The volatile spirit
of conversation or alcohol, fixed and channeled
into the axis a crystal form. Apart, the trance-
like life of plants. The cats' indirections
and sleep, troubled by strange irritabilities.
Into speech, but this is not speech, couldn't
be imagined spoken. Phantasmal sea-surge,
some nocturnal bird, wave-form of insects.
Meeting the anxious self, cruel task-master
superego—altogether unformulated, gazing
for years on end at his reflection in that pool.
A green light lingering in the west, after mauve
unmentioned. Penalties of self-abuse

    laceration of the forehead and temples.
    Three women, like Mary & co. before the tomb,
    shine their phones at a frog on the walk.
    Halcyon voices vernal hours already
    on the wing. World before her a page
    of fair ciphers, of doubtful import. Altogether
    unformulated, reflective. Exquisite fittings,
    in sumptuous fitting rooms, as if the sun
    tied the island down in bands of pink
    and orange, for the night of whipping rains.

A thin grey cloud, startled green of moss
and rarest mistletoe. Only by a more elastic

moral philosophy, more capacious mathematic,
might it all add up and come out right.
If she was a lover of strange souls, fervent watcher
of cave-shadows and antique serials,
she was a lover nonetheless. Plaintive sussurus,
breeze soughing its pneumatic vocabulary—
        building always a derivative sense
        of lives and customs, comfortable
        mythology where hamadryad, satyr,
        elf and harlequin might consort
        in lively narrative frieze. The virginal
Madonna of the Île de la Cité turns away
as the other ducks canal bridges.
Gondoliers and Columbines. Wraiths
and specters stalking Europa, stalking
the continents all. Steerpike in the kitchens,
mind's eye turned upward to the turret room.
The best of this kind are but shadows,
emending the grammar of the sprawl,
meatspace, the *hoi polloi*. Broken pillar
                and sneer of command—level sands, if
                you can bear the rhyme. A red Solo
                cup, Coca-Cola's reflective slick
                dimpled by a single sheltie hair.
                Potato chips, Chips Ahoy, faint aroma
                of dogshit. Sifts of books—classics,
        history, archaeology, the occasional *Playboy*.
        The breakers sound suspicious tonight, some bewildered
        bird in the distance. Enculturated in words

and endless entangled stories, broken and almost
mended, she would have brought home
that kitten, grey in the light as in the dark.

77. *Odysseus and the Sirens*

The curves and angles
        never fail to satisfy
the eye. Machined precision
        or splattered blurred

spontaneity. Sidewalk heat
        from six stories
below sun wan
        through smoke

glass. Billing error.
        Check misdated
and interest accrued.
        Whiff of ganja

in the hired car.
        Little red bump
of an ingrown hair.
        Fœtor of long-

unwashed dishes.
        A dervish-dance
atop the landfill stepped
        pyramid of réfuse.

Stumbled into
        the shambles
of the present
        amusement park

broken glass half-
        eaten hot dogs.
Curves and angles
        sketches and fully-

realized oils. Darkened
        rooms for fragile
works on paper.
        Camel-hair miniatures

behind glass.
        When the temperature
drops the streets smell
        less noisome.

Sounds gradually
        returning voices
traffic construction.
        Two small leashed

dogs in paroxysms
        as a cat darts
across their path.
        Insistent itch

around the rectum.
        Online auction
collectibles home furnishings
        art. Storefront

open all night all wares
        available to all.
The wavelength some
        say spreads

the virus. Bare arms
        masked faces. Scent
of soap and fæces
        under the fingernails

red marks on the bum.
        I'll take your emotion
recollected in tranquility
        and raise you a hard

gem-like flame. The red
        square is fire the black
square our souls.
        Separate the work

from the text the worker
        from her hands'
products. Political signs
        in every front

lawn a flag in every
        lapel. The curves and
angles bear us a long
        way charm us along.

78. *Language Lab*

How do I translate this word? Is it
ache, or *pain*, or *throbbing*, or *insistent*
sense of unbelonging abjection?
Broken letter of admittance, fine
receding prospect: a walled garden
viewed from hands and knees.
Shifts of scale, proportion, letter sent
from freckled shoulders to distant
knees. Under the thrums of helicopter
blades scent of new roses to chilly
disinfected corridors. That month
with only one set of shoes, and that
month among the flowers
and ornamental cacti. A lifetime ago—
two, three. Generations ranked
and gone to seed. The day's datum
sprawls down, effaces attention.
Distraction a way of life, way
of thinking, or not. There cannot be too much
attention, too much *hilaritas*. Cheer,
not quite *gaudium*, but akin enough.
Worth working out, the sequence of dates
and places, counts down to a final
whoreson zed. Null set. Humphry Davy
in Xanadu, "Ozymandias" printed
on the wings of a new-hatched
butterfly, in blood no less. Points
to connect, connections pondered
or invented: two by two, in order

of cleanness. Stopgap steps:
holiness to wholeness, priest to poet,
paradise to political nowhere,
Original Sin to the nameless crime
of existing. Progress not to be
charted, only inferred, though
his prose's formality is not at all
chilly or stiff. Stoic by nature
though nature might as well
have made him an aesthete. Conclusions
diametrically opposed, arrived at
from identical warrants. Festal
odors, whiskey enough to fill
the bathtub—but only when past
the age of drinking. "Love is Enough"
a sweatshirt motto. Be best
of all possible worlds, as if
alternatives existed. Akin enough.
Draw across, betray, bewray,
stitching new skins for old
spirits. How should I translate
this phase, this word? Paducah
on the broad Miskatonic,
to sorting files and charts
in Salieri's palace. Snow clear
to the balcony upstate, like
Siberia. Monterey surf Dostoevskian
drumbeat. Conjugating verbs,

to trace precisely out those Greekish
letters; nouns unrecognized or declined.
How do I translate this broken
letter, this broken book? A "broken
arch," a curve of missed
opportunities. Charts and files
shortwave transmissions across
the dial, Luzon to Meißner.
*Voyna i mir, De Bello Paceque, Krieg
und Frieden,* files and charts,
tests, assessments, CAT scans
and MRIs. A new year, new harvest
of leaves to rake and bag. How
do I translate *we are not holpen?*

79. *Water-Cannons*

a glass spilled across
        the table top moment
of horrifying embarrassment
        replayed over and over
again never to draw
        attention never to have
eyes upon me in that
        way avoiding center
stage the family ethos
        a mistimed echo
humiliating misunderstanding
        directions baring myself
literally before the class's
        knowing snickers dream
of unexpected nakedness

"Longwood" indeed—four hundred
        acres of trees, elms, oaks,
rhododendrons, ponds and streams
        the "English" garden, artificially
natural, rectilinear "Italian" pools,
        fountains to rival Versailles,
conservatory that never seems
        to end—the eye-pulling blue
of Wyeth's *Island Funeral* from those chemical
        vats, bubbling from a ferment
of black powder, the corpses
        of uncounted deer, natives,

powder cloud carrying aloft
two hundred thousand souls
over those four years. The waterworks
spout, interweave, to the sound
of Lennon's dismal piano
"Imagine." The cannonades
are only water. Water hoses
in Birmingham, chemical agents
in the District, holding as always
unread aloft a Bible.
Cannon-shots counting
down this last fortnight:
the woman huddles bare-armed
with her little daughter,
with her mother, under the cloud
of droplets, laughs Russian.

the Milky Way a gleaming
leprosy across the black
rush of vomit into an unfolded
garrison cap fluid quick
with white larvae of stars
fog creeps into the headlight
beams surround suffused
with white a light in darkness
in a dark place which is
the world entire

"a monstrous tide of competing,
fleeting existence"—a constant
feed, unending cycle. Not to be
added to, multiplied.
World already the world's
simulacrum, needing no
mimesis, imitation, propagation.
The flying moment of grace, struck down
on paper—harmonic movement, chime
of vowels and stresses—why separate
it out from the incessant flickering
of such moments across his senses'
screen (he wondered)? The grass
at his feet producing more beauty
in an instant than his lifetime
could hope to capture.
That Russian laugh,
eyes crinkled at the corners, curves
of her upper arms, abject
joy of the child. Water-cannons
of money, credit, slippery wastage
of spectacle—droplets fracture
the late afternoon sun
into—what else?—a rainbow.
Moment to be set down, against
his will, against the ruins
of us all—set down
still. It is good be glazed
with water

in the late afternoon sun,
to laugh at water dancing
over a bed of black
powder, chemical agents.
This is good, this is
enough. This is all
there is, the monstrous tide.

80.

It was not an angel that spoke
to me from the flame crown
of that tree, but the spirit
of the tree itself. And the paper
unfolded itself to receive
these words, the tongues of autumn:

They were counting, and counting, and marking
their tallies on big sheets of paper at the front
of the room. A show of hands, guilty or innocent.
The hemlock, or a lifetime's free meals
at the senatorial canteen. Yellow haze
in the bottle, faint tinge of lemon
on the palate. Tingle of cannabis
through my limbs. The narcosis
of warm stout. We were watching the midnight
movie at Cornell Cinema, back
from touring the collegetown bars:
a tightly-plotted, complex thriller, crammed
with technological twists. Whose attention could follow
that?—certainly not mine, head wuzzy
with drink—but I was gripped with anxiety,
feared for the fate of the protagonist
and her handsome, gormless sidekick
as they tumbled from one predicament
to another, even deeper. Worse yet, the absolute
disconnect from one scene to the next,
like that classic film of Elizabeth

and Mary Queen of Scots I saw at seven
or eight, short-sightedly couldn't tell
one bewigged, beruffed, glittering monarch
from the other. Two hundred thirty-
seven, a woman marks on a big sheet
of paper at the front of the room.
You were next to me in the movie, sprawled
diagonally across your seat, head
on my shoulder. Your hair smelled of shampoo,
beer, and cigarettes. A nice smell.
And suddenly, as the subway car
on the screen shot down the tunnel,
passengers screaming and praying,
the anxiety just drained away—who was that
up there, what was happening? how will I
finish that term paper, make next month's
rent? where, after all, are we going?
—and I breathed in the smell, deeply, touched
your face, my fingers slick with popcorn butter.
Three hundred forty-two, a woman marks
on a big sheet of paper—a screen—
at the front of the room. One queen
is red-haired like the Queen of Hearts,
the other red-haired as the Queen of Diamonds.
How was I to choose, know which
was destined for the block, which
for the coinage?

No more change for the touchless terminal,
no tokens for the bus. No free rides. They're
moving down the car checking receipts.
Not a roller-coaster we were on, a subway car,
flashing past stations, flashing past
other cars. An express, we'd thought at first,
but even an express stops somewhere.
Not moving but being moved, voice
always passive, rate and velocity
at another's command. Taking charge
only a dream of youth, dream
from when we wore knickerbockers
and pinafores. The day after
tomorrow acres away,
an unwritten book. Marred
already, water-rippled, mud-stained.
The pictures you hid between the pages
of the thickest, most obscure encyclopedia
volume, the tell-tale grass
clippings your mother found inside
your cast-off underpants.
Write this down in a book, said the angel,
but the letters fade as I write them,
as the pen lifts from the paper
to strike down the next word. I am
lost, unsure, I cannot read the words
of this script handed to me,
and my phone is dead. If an angel
spoke to me from a flaming-red

tree, would I understand its speech?
        If it spread its six horrible rainbow
        wings, gathered its iridescent robes
        in scornful parting, how could I imprint
that sight on my faithless memory?
Every messenger is terrible, and no news is the only
tidings around which my twisted tongue can curl.

81.

It was a "ghost walk" we were on, through
the old town, stumbling over tree-roots and cobbles,
reaching for our phone lights and then
refraining, loath to spoil the gaslit
atmosphere. The guide was talking,
voice rising to a murmur and dropping
to a whisper—beaten wives
who'd cooked their husbands in pastries,
tormented apprentices who poisoned
their masters' after-dinner tankards,
slaves, crippled or blinded, who never
saw redress or revenge. The ground crackled
with brittle bones, specters stalked
the parade ground or skulked dim alleys.
Hauntology, someone said, trying to make
a Nineties joke, and I heard *Ontology*, even older
and lamer stab at wit. Hard to distinguish,
in this light—the only light I have—memory
from haunting. I remember
the past. The past haunts me.

It is a presentation manuscript, initials illuminated,
quotations written in red ink. The parchment
is very fine and thin. The artist in the scriptorium
worked well, her letters remarkably regular and legible
across the evenly ruled lines. Only a handful
of erasures, deftly made. The marginal notes—
as notes tend to be on such sumptuous
manuscripts—are as carefully written

as the text itself, though in smaller characters;
the extent to which they take exception to,
even argue with, the text is striking.
Turning its pages, or even gazing on a single leaf,
one is transported to the far-off moment
when it was written, to a room lit only
by natural light, or the inconstant glimmer
of candles, to a patient hand—once graceful,
perhaps—copying word after word, pausing
at moments to dip her quill in an inkwell,
at more distant intervals wiping the pen
clean, laying it aside to dry and be sharpened,
beginning again with a new instrument.
The text, though, is the same—lines unfolding
from left to right behind the moving hand—
the lineal descendent, ten centuries on,
of some single ur-text, a gleaming
vision hovering over her as she patiently
writes. NCIPIT, she writes at the head
of a page, leaving a rectangular space
for the illuminated I. And neatly, many
pages later, her EXPLICIT—in slightly smaller
letters—hovers two-thirds down the leaf,
itself a leaf, trembling and tentative, as if
to be blown loose in an autumnal wind,
soaked and softened by rain, tumbled, trodden
underfoot, received into the shifting
and shelving archive-mounds of word-stuff,
slowly sifting into compost.

Year of the Crucified Panda, zone
of the Headless Sun, water slapping
against the walled banks—Pont
Mirabeau, half a century gone—
a bridge, a handshake—whose hand
before mine?—a gangplank
from one boat to an unseen other,
unaddressed, undirected bottle-writing—
naming the bridges, the water-towers,
the portals and gratings—words
like stelae or pebbles, proper names
word effaced stubborn in vagueness
and random specificity—cattle-lists
of Linear-B enthralling the eye
with their ligatures and serifs, names
of God in uncountable variations

> the van rattled across the bridge, almost
> waking you, I heard the piled boxes
> in back shift and settle—crammed
> with forty years' papers, electric and cable
> bills, pay stubs, grocery receipts, every
> blessed one of my mother's weekly letters—
> hoped, for more than a moment, the doors
> would jar open, empty the lot into the river
> below, clear space for some new
> beginning—*incipit vita nova*, something
> like that, *went down to the ships*, or
> *A round of fiddles*—a beach hoedown,

under unnaturally bright sun—grease
traced on the limestone, planed flat, plaited hatch-
work of lines, masses—to shake that hand,
nails grimy crescent moons, callused
and nicked from the bound steel edges
and labor-shining handles of the craft—
a single callus on the middle finger, nails
closely pared and buffed—missing
a finger, the drummer moves tentatively, follows
the guitar just a moment behind,
the One is elusive, slips away, can't
quite be grasped—the signature lives
in every line, etched, scribbled,
smeared—the water wrinkles the page,
the ink rises in coils from the paper
like smoke in the liquid—the pads
of the fingers raisin-wrinkled,
color leaching away—no fingerprints
on the bottle, no words on the scrolled
sheet—unsilent depths, swayed by the slow
metronome of oceanic dub, sea
of dub, embracing bottom end
of bass without bottom, abyssal
marine flower or no-floor, no-one's-floor,
no-one's-flower—the myriad petals
floating and turning, tangled in floating
hair—brown, golden, ashen watery pale.

82.

Nothing was quite right, nothing
was thankful. Nothing was good
enough for us. We gave thanks
to nothing, for nothing. Squabbled
on the train, playing cards over a cooler
of export ale, throwing down
the cards when we'd won a hand, when
we'd lost a hand. Is that two or three
lights diagonal back beyond the garage,
or do my glasses need adjusting?
The money flows away, sheets out
like money does. Not enough airplane
noise overhead these days. They present
themselves, the beautiful pair, once again
a newly reconciled quirky sorority. Hairnets
and all, they were ladling out provisions
from behind the steam tables. Unidentified
    stew, but savory, vegetables boiled
free of vitamins and color. Three weeks
    on from the new dispensation, new
testament. The line stretched out before us,
    behind us as well. Waiting, a nervous
energy. Passive tension. Enough as good
    as a feast, my mother said;
I hear her voice still, unsure of her
    pronunciation. Attention the natural
    prayer of the soul—Malebranche,
    through Benjamin to Celan. Handshake,
    message in a bottle—Mandelstam,

for whom a poem most definitely
made something happen. Something
happened, something became something
else, or nothing in particular, and the timbre
of the air, smell of the birdsong,
changed, became sour and odd.

A Memorable Fancy; or, a conversation
in the garden, around the fire-pit:
The angel said that time was up, that time
was almost over, that we'd overstayed
our welcome. It was a letter informed
us the payment was overdue, the power
would be shut off within days. The furnace, I said,
is oil. He: But the thermostat's electric,
so there's a problem there. The fall
had descended with a vengeance, bags
and bags of leaves to be raked, burned,
bagged. Always a smell of smoke,
woodsmoke, tobacco, leaves, ganja.
Life is a journey of new discovery,
he said, a continual broadening
of horizons. That sounds (I said)
karmicly wonderful, but I'd rather
drill down where I already stand,
what with the night coming and all.
If time's almost up, who wants
to be reading the user's manual
for some new appliance

when the buzzer sounds? Not "taking in sail"
        so much—ahoy!—just working
harder where one's already invested
        the sweat equity. And after all,
you can probably have it both ways—
        if you're fortunate enough, that is,
to have it at all.

Thanks for nothing, that's what the bus driver
said as we nodded and thanked him. Someone said
the subways were running again, but no one
I knew wanted to descend those greasy stairs,
breathe that miasmal air. So it was a bus
we were on—a crosstown special, or an airport
express. Somehow we'd managed the tight
turn, lumbering over a curb, just missing
a knot of pedestrians. An opening we were on
our way to, a gala, a show to take us—
however briefly—out of the weather, cold
biting the scabs on our knuckles, the milia
clustered beneath our eyes, out of our selves.
Last year's gala was pink, and camp,
and kind of butch—great fun. This time
around everything's as black and white
as an old television episode, and we're
turning in circles, like the hands of a clock,
a hank of hair circling the drain.
Piano cycling through the same four
chords, saccharine strings—no bass,

no wobble, no dub—metronomic
ticking, funneling us all spaced
out and covered into the same
dark and narrow house.

83.

I.

Prologue, to begin, patron-addressing, notable suck-
up—the round oratorical instrument, invocation
aid-seeking. Leafmeal dapple patterned, owlish
oracular. Bare thrust, trap door and flies, final
baiting. Stage to be set, robes ready aired
and donned. Plexiglass curtain between driver
and fare, for the cunning romance of mediated
temperance. Slipshod for chilblains, creakage
of the wood, the word. Megaphone in mask,
concealment rooting latest intestinal strife.
He mulls rancor, steeps gratitude. Ridges
of his forehead coil and welcome serpentine.
Eight days' oil, the stewed flesh of Mizraim.

II.

Noëmi or Ruth, Margarete or Shulamith,
Queen and concubines. Orchards, promenades,
asemic order of landscaped architectures.
Reedy, broken bended in the wind, round oratorical
under the Western sun. Flame-lances and mounted
flamingos; rainbow bridge, Calais à Dover. That was
a way of thinking it, snarled and outright, that was
the Autumn Lands, end of all singing. What throngs
mead-hall pollard, why dissemble disadvantaged
optics? Bilious entry, violoncello or doubled bass.
The Blind Boys groan Jesus, martyrs gnash Baal.
Tenacity ambiguous, alone. Word made flash-
drive thumbs its path humbly, abrogated.

III.

Tenacious, reedy, broken or bent. Not to be rent
from one bolt, subjected to the discipline
of aleatory. Provoked invocation, *vox dei*
or *vox clamantis,* Nabis arrested in bewildered
wandering. Cyan sands. Salmon, mauve, the huge
hues of Levantine Eos. Dub factory, dub
plantation. Parabolic hinge, the parseable
distinction—*so that* and *because.* Risible
causation. Megaphone in mask. To prologue,
provocation. Singed forge, sheared hair. Panoply
aggrandize, for procession aptly penitent
to volume ladage. Fuzz and tremelo and envelope
filter, harbinger on wing rampant windy dark.

IV.

Not too satisfactory, bitter scent of burnt peanut
and offal on the wind, over airwaves. Behind
the plexiglass curtain, bamboo screen. Oratorical
screed, rounded periods and i's dotted
with winsome hearts. Dayglo hair, La Brea
spa session. No proper structure, or improper
structure. Begin anywhere, goddess. Sing or
make me sing, make me like it. Siren-song
to ignore lyric blockage. Query unanswerable
just how fucked are *we* implicit blockage.
Siren behind plexiglass. Psyche behind eyes, butterfly
lashes, birches ripe with buds. Pneuma behind
thorax, goodly-greaved dominatrix capital.

V.

Reservoir ducks, leadless dogs. An accent
incontrovertible, searing joinery—my hands,
my eyes! Condition, have it, of the universal
penal visiting room. Mimed embraces, mimed
acclaim. Rounded, oratorical, bamboo.
Traces maculate spray the backsplash, newly
replenished: burnt peanut, to fired Portuguese
ceramic. Decorative knotwork siren-
song. NO FARMERS NO FOOD in turbanned
hooting caravan. Involuntary unhappy
tonsure, the pity, a beaded waterclock
snakes around the forearm. Novitiate
dominatrix, she rolls her eyes ecstatic.

VI.

Talcum anthrax baking soda cut dioxin
and other exotica to bring back the good old
days; fireflash and fraternity torqued round
the renal axis to "responsibility." Size matters,
vagueness matters, the precision of oversight
recovered. Queenly concubines, Noëmi and Gretl
speaking a slipshod prologue—rounded, oratorical.
Vox Clamantis. Mizraim the reed shaken.
Unwinds himself from the wrappers, unguent
dripping, urgency of message. He stinks obviously.
Point emphasized in all variations, narrated
across stematta. This is after all peak
Christology, magic cannon gender reveal.

VII.

Every premised descent followed by overrapid
easier, ivory, more expeditiously managed
return to the waters and battlefields. Nostos over,
foreknowledge or flashback—now to the grind
of evisceration and countermarch. Fragrant oil
over entrails offered, hymns loud and unlovely.
Alien corn prologue to colonial homecoming, stage-
clearing: new colors, patterns, properties.
Pious equals decent, equals dutiful. Decorum
obsolescent, quorum inadvertently crowd-
sourced. Barks aflame, keels sinuous as nymphal
spines, white people and white sow. Overwritten
ancestral justification poisonous eddy outward.

VIII.

Song in the scriptorium. Serifs and descenders, scrolls
vomited and re-eaten. Turning over in latexed
hands, oily with shiny millennial labors.
Panic theory, agency panic breathing
close quarters shoulder by jowl, so that
every jot and tittle forethought arrest
intended. Ariade–Arachne lines spun
so fine they vanish to the naked eye,
shimmer peripheral or dazzle in oblique
casement sunray. A paucity of motifs.
No imagination whatsoever weaves the
Liffy and the Styx, androbovine mongrel
gnawing a collarbone at bare center.

IX.

Shaken reed, bent but unbroken. *Vox*
clamantis from the whirlwind or unburnt
burning bush. Founding Fathers in technicolor,
or handy portable bronze. Historical primer
in mnemonic hexameter, temporality
in music. Dated artefacts measure out
stunned distances from the polis's founding,
style *AUC*. Coming attractions will unroll
a seven-sealed scroll of heroic self-denial.
Strange gods from over the rivers, brought home
in olive duffle-bags and leopard carry-ons.
Uninnoculated body politic, surfing swells
of fever and chill, out of anyone's depth.

X.

Prologue: invocation. Catalogue, senses objects
tints hues noises impressions timbres documents
names modes of transportation. Round, oratorical.
Auratic: hieratic. Altar incense obscurity billows
mystery. Uninitiate. Late unlettered abstraction,
car park sausage machine. How tortuous to say
when sudden merge, the hard merge, obliges.
At her rostrum the orator is avatar of the back-
wards dark, dopey cartoon angel arisen out a tangle
of random lines. Only connect said the scion
of empire, on ballfield. Complexion athwart,
oar butting nymphal spine and rib cage, and how long
must one carry one's father through the ruined night?

84. *Aisthesis*

The curves emerged when the pieces
came right sketched graphite
bleeds up through the oils
receding green depths boskage stagnant
waters watery light interior hefts
antecedent barter hauteur of gaze
instep emphatic edenic couture aright
awry emphatic gaze regal repulsive
invitational altar call sloping dimpled
altar marbled cleft darker boskage

like a labyrinth he proposed
the succession of emphatic single
impressions parataxis presentment
drowned cathedral crowded ranks
of fellows' handwork rising up
into distant high shadows
seascape sunrise steerage composing
themselves the lines against sky
vault aligned intention repose
emphatic gaze from bosky labyrinth

shimmery linen laid paper network
aligned minute unemphatic grasp
slippery gaze arrest or reproof
letters twigs haired tendrils mazing
the surface into untended ripples
ruth alien corn queenly asp
limbs in under linen rumple

drapery curves emerged when pieces
aright hauteur of gaze aside
edenic couture spray of leaves

trainers membered bikes flag early
completion man's first disobedient
arms topless burning equine gift
queenly asp to regal breast
apotropaic turn about luxurious
east silks exotica sliding emphatic
gaze against marble altars
desire of the eyes pride of life
pulses' counted number sharpens
wonderfully concentrated succession

white as marble cadaver much
hewn from Tuscan hillsides
desire of life under capital
sentence hard gem-like the phrase
sodden trainers ungainly weather
the flock altogether disorient
that eastern queen domestic
concubinage curls coil asp-like
in oil-light forty winters out
older than the hide-bound rocks

counted bridges telephone poles
lowering clouds rising mesas
westward the course the regatta

eastern flags alien yellow corn
labyrinth occluded uncovered winding
in every sense androbovine
mechanical coupling changed
in the telling oral to secondary
narratological forms shaping
senses dwindle passages even

forty winters eight days' oil lines
points prick out rounded forms
curves emerge marbled altars
cenotaphs portrait busts realistic
stylized hyacinthine curls coiled
asp-like eastern queen oil-scented
Phrygian boyishness thumbprint-flakes
dissolving in rain thallocracy root
the pirates archipelago of milk
scattered shells eyes mother-of-pearl

angel hovering of ending enigmatic
smiles male and female angle
of incident variation serpentine
asp-like beast-headed romp
of deities eastern queen wallowed
triremes awkward incendiary
Grecian fire in thumbprint-flakes
forked tongue to regal breast queen
to knight's pawn topless towers
older than the broken stones

angel of memory that one cold
eclipsed night moon blood-red
your hair in my mouth attenuation
mnemonic linear serpentine mazy
passages of gem-like flickers
count pulsations asp-like eastern
concubinage from toppled towers
shingled sandy beaches monochrome
snap to shore angled memory
false authenticity falter data feed

towards faux fur data faulty
dates relationships askew sensation
perception paste nor jewel queenly
serpentine canvas after picture
working on paper still-wet limpet
older than rocks angle enigmatic
asemic symptomatic autonomic
rightly antinomian between betwixts
slender curves emerge a piece
rightly retrieved converse apart

green depths receding seagreen grey
serpentine nil bisecting canvas
worked out on paper squared
for transfer bisected limpid
curves emerge when pieces retrieved
askew alight linear angles
asymptotes arcs skewed unplot

axes lust of the eye prided
life pieces measured moved
blockage and regal boskage

queenly gaze ocular proof asp-like
curl across regal curve bisected
squared to transfer rough sketch
to polished ivory product blockage
linear intent not to speak
a moving picture predilection
of faltering memory succeeding
impressions grasped as concepts
gem-like counted the murmur
pulsations receding dwindle dim

trunks water boskage still-wet fabric
receding interior studio light regal gaze
triremes queenly wallow serpentine
interrogation asp-like mnemonic auroral
light temple song loud and unlovely
forget to remember blood-red moon
polished hardwood disordered futon
wood and water curves asymptote
counted gem-like blue-grey queenly
half-lidded startled asp-like curve.

85.

Who was that masked man? folded into
himself across a chair, well-worn dumpy
parka, knitted woolen gloves draped
in impatient pharaonic angles?

Fixed in his baleful, glassy eye,
his domey pate, his mariner's skinny
hand, we found ourselves—despite
ourselves—saying "we" again.

The dreaming city, pastel city, shining
city on a hill—the voice on the PA said
it was a ghost town, the boxed paragraphs
in the textbook said it was a myth.

Ruined cityscape, painted backdrop. The horses
neighed, whinnied, reared in dismay.
We stepped over broken glass plastic bottles
styrofoam, and saw the emerald towers

stone bridges over the river crowded
with boutiques and bodegas, colored
spires shifting hue as the wind changed.
A soundtrack playing around us, funky

unobtrusive, as if the whole shebang
were an elevator to some higher ground.
My hand was in yours, I wanted to make love
there and then, you wanted to take it all

in for a moment, at least take the time
to pull off our clothes, find a grassy
knoll, a bit of shadow under the trees
of the park. The Park was Manet's *Déjeuner,*

one of those kitschy salon bacchanals,
a Rochester poem. Young people
in flimsy chitons were handing out
dainty spliffs and sea-green glasses,

rumor had it there was face- and body-
painting just around the bend. Carnaval
I dreamed it, afraid at any moment
I'd accidentally click my bootheels

and wake up in sepia, grey Auntie Em
frowning down over the quilt. Wake
to find the color drained from the same
bricks, a pointy wind cutting apart

our flashy filmy robes. We said we,
we were afraid to say *hope* or *change.*
It was all change, after all, something
happening every time a screen lit up.

The lights were still the same out over
the river, pointing stupidly upward.
The same dogs sniffing and tugging,
the same uninterested cats. I held your hand,

or I held you in my hand, your face
on my phone. A land line back
to Eden, they imagined a hundred years
ago, heard the crackling voices

of far-off ancestors—fancy accents,
quaint turns of phrase and all. The girl
in her room, bathed in pulsing LEDs,
listens to her grandchildren in sixty-

second bursts. We lay there a long time
without moving, afterwards, sweat
drying on our skins. It turned dark,
there were kids with sparklers

running off to the right. Somewhere
we heard the baaing of the long-gone
sheep who gave the meadow its name,
remembered the horses on the bridle path.

("The Bridal Path," a wedding chapel—
white, of course—in deepest Tennessee,
just off the interstate, at the foot
of a hillside. A gravel parking lot.

I misremember the wishing well, I think—
which is just as well.) Still and dark
but the air was unexpectedly warm.
I thought you'd fallen asleep, whispered

your name. You said mine, then "Let's
be quiet for a while. I'm writing letters
to the dead. Telling them they're not alone.
Telling then how peaceful they can be."

So we lay there a long while, cracklings
and hissings in the distance, until the stars
came gradually out, shone so bright the trees
and cranes and buildings faded to black.

86.

Annulled, that the last moment
should spread poignant and trim
across the park. Ground
saturated, turned over salted
and moved both mechanically
and by stout navvy-like
shoulders. Behold and turn,
recognize athwart the walls
to tower beside the trench.

Palms shiver unaccustomed, bare
to arctic alienation. Memories
of five years past melt
with the patchy afternoon thaw.
Her figure broken on the slates,
horror palpitant through veils
of distance. The branches
oblique shagged emitting
light, deflecting or prisming.

Turn to behold, a Turner
seascape of crystal, casting
of crowns and outgrown carapaces.
Worn through and soft, fabric reluctant
to pull away from sanguine hairs.
The child hurled, centaur *in extremis*—
ignorance always bears ambiguous
gifts which charity welcomes
out of tumid saturation.

Thunder-broken on the parapet,
swallowed in earth, gnawing
rival's cheek-flesh. Samurai
dishonored beyond compromise,
memory of Hibernian geisha
aggravated, raw. Filmic measure,
bardic cross-cuts and wide-angle
panoramic, names of the fallen
hasting by like union credits.

The pack pulls asunder, differently
instincted. Copper stubble of Malcolm's
scalp, Martin's face emphatic wedge.
Earth did not open, nor seers were
swallowed up with poltroons. Feces
smeared across marble pavings,
tribal and triumphant. The arc
ought be everlasting, bending
as predictable as the bridle path.

The city's spirit, robed and regal,
would appear as you cast the dice.
Crossing rivers, by no means canceling
aleatory. Narrative extended travelogue
or broken vacation. Vacant commercial
boarded gaze. The jab releases
pent-up desires, to liberate or flatly
saturate, as the brush saturates
pigment on the third go-round.

Why scheme your stay, why bend
so ardently that arc? The curves
the slattern frost makes ejected
from the shovel's surface, chunk
of pile on terrace. Flakes
shine or flicker in the porch-light's
cone, darkness even darker.
The sophistication of knowing things
is a stupid, sordid final prize.

Portrait *a vicious libel* on orchre
as icon leaf. Round glitter or glass,
black trousers white whippet elegance.
Copper stubble unshaven imperiality.
First among equals always implied,
what more could sway the fall
of drapery across marble shoulder
or polished bronze gluteus?
Aquatint proof etched against time.

Graphic work and pencilled violence.
The sleep of reason both demands
and produces ornaments of daylight.
Common tongue hyperbole. Over the top,
the dialectic scrambles in stop-motion
jerks. Grovels in mud, assigns
its darker brother the reins. Casques
of spun carbon fiber, horsehair
scrapes rosin from tender cuirasses.

Passionate intensities, finger
gestures from *The King and I*, periodic
renewal of the art in public veins.
Leather supple, sole broken straight
across. Grand struggle as usual
over the scraps, Lazarus french-kissing
Dives on widescreen. My people
proud of nothing but their salvation,
blood-laundered by prolonged scansion.

Cold night closes particularity,
animated scamper. Gem-lights
to the east, deities of spectacle
and money. Bloody knuckles taped,
as you tape the marginal areas.
Blue-grey on cream, ochre tending
to warm yellow, always crimson.
Curves determine beauty in all
its variations. Rectilinearity aside.

Hysterical misery to ordinary
unhappiness: the endless talking cure,
words unwinding across the page,
the streets, the parks. Walks, parterres,
civic pools shoaled with snow. Capaneus
denied deity, a descending fireball; pious
Amphiaraus, for whom earth opened.
As if the ground had ever been solid.
Curves, cracks, pornographic entrances.

Brake-squeals horn-rages to mechanical
Aufhebung, bird's- or god's-eye
panorama. Distended cheeks, touched
with boyish pink, of Mantegna's trumpets.
Annulled, the blue-grey pigment spread
in third wash go-round. Clotted knuckles,
crumpled tape. Liquid sheeting divests
pavers and slate. Shovel away, navvy,
at commodity's glistening drifts.

87. *A Brief History of Epic Memory*

The way the light flashes the rim
of a tumbler, triggering the mind
to recall a similar flash, perhaps
years ago—the synaptic short-circuit
that floods one with déjà vu,
the sense the mouse scuttling
under the backyard grill in the icy
night has scuttled, in just that
shivery manner, before one's eyes
before. The automaton rhythm
beneath the rave, the hobnailed
hexameter, the cicadas'
clicking of resurrection. First time
tragedy, second time farce, thereafter
tradition. Cannibalistic patricide;
then measured ritual; then culture.

The sea-wandering hero will come home
to his patient wife; or found,
after unnumbered trials, a new home;
or will be stabbed ignominious and steaming
in the bath by his wife's paramour.
Achilles chooses a short life and undying
fame; Ulysses settles into middle-aged
conjugality, dies at the hands
of an unsuspected by-blow, sails
to wrack at the base of Purgatory Isle.
I'm afraid of the sea, even the mild chop
off Fire Island, the Gulf Coast's languid

lap. Hard to imagine the audacity
to put out beyond the Pillars—at least
for some land-locked Ionian auditor.

First time tragedy, second time epic.
Roving adventures of some eponymous
hero, of the commodity form, of the articles
of speech. The alpha, Romanized, between
two ts on Golgotha—in one fanciful
reading—the serpent watching from the left,
matter itself (*'ule*) turning its back
to the right. The word invites fanciful
interpretation, as does the world—arranged,
Ruskin believed, for our convenience
and pleasure. Outworn tale of the tribe.
At this stage the only common stories
are dark narratives of betrayal, cabals
in shadow. Monetary trades. Lines
on graphs, charting our designed
obsolescence. The girl, hair glowing
an unnatural but pleasing auburn,

echoed in the polished belly
of an upright bass, cradled

in the printed records of all cultures,
listens to a lecture on the Stamp Act.

Her attention is as usual divided,
between the woman talking

on the laptop screen and the news
on her phone—a new draconian

inevitably to-be-challenged abortion law
in a southern state. All is as usual

in crisis. There are no snakes curling
from the white pods in her ears: the oracle

speaks over Bluetooth these days. The books
pressing their weight around her are dusty,

spend their ancestral energies collecting
more dust. *The photograph*, the voice says,

*is not mountains and valleys, dunes
and hills, but the dust breeding*

on the surface of the Large Glass.
Dust, I remember, is evidence

of Original Sin. (*There is no dust,*
Mother Ann Lee said to her acolytes sweeping,

in Heaven.) The sin itself,
according to our notes, has been

identified in quasi-Hegelian form,
a lacuna in the recordings of the Founding

Fathers. The trains are running on time
again, the buses—as usual—can't

be relied on. Tomorrow, or the next day,
maybe the next week, sometime soon,

we'll sweep the dust from the shelves
and corners, erase the whole

topography so elaborately reported
in Books Six and Seven, the circles

and bolges and subterranean descents.
There are ways down, said the wise

orangutan, quoting both Virgil and Dante.
First time tragedy, second time miniseries,
thereafter franchise. I own electric gardening
tools, it seems, mostly to demonstrate
my skill at cutting extension cords.
The commodity form is our Atropos,
brusque umbilicus-shearing
obstetrician. You cut the land line
to Eden with the roto-tiller, trying
to make that patch of back garden
a little Versailles. The topless cell

towers have burnt, they've rolled
the shutters down across the book-
cases. Epic memory ends here.

88.

I.

Minarets cloud-capped towers
slowly dissolving into slush half-
grasped concept half-remembered
place-names. Raw spring early
but late-feeling. Safe and effective
the single-strike enters a crowded
field course thick with mourning
doves and barking dogs. Every catalogue
an epic catalogue manifesto
or shipping manifest list
of contents spilt discontented.
Representation elected or appointed.
The number fluctuate nor do they
lie. Neither do they spin. Fortnight
out instruments agreeing overprecise
forecasting to administrative metrics.
Lie still a moment actuarial data
will soothly give a ballpark idea.
Siren-songs of ordinary moment
self-selecting diurnal placatory hum.

II.

Manifests gone down full fathom
five coffined Mariana. Raw barebacked
the man of the hour flexes winces.
That was no mechanical bull
the waitresses in chaps and thongs
but veritable fire-eyed Minotaur.

Nothing in excess implies a passionate
discipline sensual abnegation.
Colors strong tastes fester eschewed
and the hand breezes off the breakers
bell. Lie you still move not
from against me scant satisfaction
of pad-footed withdrawal.
Thousand ships by their flotillas
captains and divine genealogies.
Like the branches of an evergreen
broken under the weight of snow
so broken. Wound catalogues weapons
manifest. Blessing breeze through
layers of fabric animal skins.

III.

Self-knowledge interminable analysis
talking no-cure. Scoop out the middle
exercising peripheral muscles boost
extremities. Twilight deity
first veiled then singular to simply
phantasmal. Teeth rattled suspension
manifests. Epic catalogue available
twenty-four hours universally
translated. Lie still passion spent
what indeed could be smoother
more pleasant? Blocks of sound
molded gauntlet. More pity
for the shapes on the screen.

Immaterial cathexis kinship
relations proffered or chosen.
A range broader far than the quotidian.
All too soon the deadline descent
of the final curtain. Hamadryads
and neon fauns prance off
stage left or through the audience.

IV.

Gods of the gloaming little roadside
shrines. Backfill as back-story. Data
dump profluent reception bewilderment.
Turn and behold *noli me tangere*
finger in actual flesh. Aphrodite
leaks ichor angels crushed beneath
their own armor. At a certain point
names fail enumeration takes
over. Epic catalogue to epic
spreadsheet. Springbok slaughtered
oxen by the drove. Trench wall
parapet. The noumenal *what is*
the scree of montaged appearances.
Figures of the scree. The eye altering
adumbrates prolegomenon critique.
Virtue ethics defunct signaling
the Party of God under siege
yet again headline infinitely recycled.
Immaterial cathexis fading almond-
eyed naiads slyly grinning fauns.

V.

Frigid ether whets the blinding beams.
Wind a train in the tunnel smearing
ambient noise In the cold the One
beats a hibernal retreat shelter
with dead gods. Snow drops
any day now. Manifest return
of forest deities under asphalt
slush. Incoming broadly
read incommensurable material
cathexis. Sap rising. Fluctuant
measurements suit variable foot
whose spring is all too painfully
accurate. Please tell me softly
when to stop lest we gain
the upper hand and mercy rain
down. Dissolving the clear
outlines into slush. Rotteth
away. Light blue windbreaker
barely worn and worn thing
rubbed to a memorial film.

VI.

The absent and anyway impossibles
are not our parents and vice-
versa. The earth never opened
for oracular bones and voice
opens inarticulate. Inward
defilement sepulchral camouflage

decorum outward outworn. A way
of saying it outmoded trans-
atlantic. Finical orthography
of gesture garb and address
sodden hoodie under bespoke
blazer. The earth opens promiscuously
with parental generosity. Spongy
thaw a mere stumble would set awry.
Hamadryads fauns naiads all that
mythological shit coiled like dog-
droppings beneath a grey snowbank.
Stumbled fell bruised myself
in wrath and embarrassed age.
Lie still old thing in my fretfulness.

89.

fallen petals clot the aphalt
air vivid confused
with a dozen birdsongs'
cross-conference
imagined colors imagined
presences bent superflux
hyaline radical tangle
of furred ear or goat's-
beard in the leggy thorns
birdsong or reed-pipes
the same three or four
notes random order intervals
plangent complaint gives way
to goatfoot celebration
and back again

morning world
morning behind every
treebud and bulb
tentative dew trembles
beneath emphatic light
mauve diffuses
into pink the sun's
rim just breaking
the water
morning
of the world
slipping almost
entirely out of

memory presences
        in every bush and bent
green leaf every
        tree and snarl
of clutching ivy
        burn last night's rain
from the flagstones
        the concrete breaks
into my eyes
        a fierce loving
blur we only read
        about those days
our great-grandparents wandered
        in many-layered old-fashioned
woolens and flaxes maybe
        entirely naked through
the green morning

Writing again? she said, and *what*
are you writing? I'm writing
fan fiction, imagining what happens
after the end of the book, what went on
before the book begins. I'm gathering
all the author interviews and all the posts
on the discussion boards, I'm weaving
them together into a giant story
that tells all the stories the book
didn't tell. An endless book, spilling
over scrolls and scrolls, webpage after webpage.

Each chapter begins with an epigraph
from an obscure song of the Seventies,
long before you were born. There are holes
in the records, lacunae—spaces where the fine
cross-hatch work has faded with time, has been
smeared or rubbed away, where the figures
can no longer be made out clearly. Sometimes
a historian mentions a battle on a peninsula
long ago washed away; an art historian,
praising one masterpiece, describes another
we've never seen; a scholiast, illustrating
some quaint regional usage, quotes two lines
of an otherwise lost epic—and those two lines
hint at a story that changes everything.

We want to hear that story, we want to know
how it comes out. That's what my fan fiction
will do, that's why it needs to be long
and longer still, why it needs to be
stretched out and taken up by someone else
when I can't type anymore. There can't be any
holes in the story, there can't be any blank spaces
on the maps, the fine-grained line work must go
to the very edge of every illustrated page, into
the gutter and beyond. I'm writing a world,
you see, all the oceans, continents, and mountains
in it, all the kingdoms and republics and great swathes
of debated nomadic territory, the fawns and hamadryads
and seamonsters and deities and demigods, and all

the bare forked poorly individuated homunculi
living therein. It has no genre, this world, neither
epic nor realistic, too sordid for tragedy and too sad
for comedy. It's hard-boiled space-opera, or pulp
sword and sorcery. No bestseller, but the book for whose sake
the world exists. Scripture and canon both,
both text and commentary, and ground
for future commentaries, redactions, revisions,
sequels and wholesale rewritings.

        evening work—they set us
to copying, by the swaying bulbs
        of the freight cars, lading lists
and rosters, ink fading and writing
        crabbed, at places entirely
illegible; eyeskips common,
        misreadings commoner, they
wanted every last mark of insertion
        and grumpy marginal
scribble reproduced precisely,
        as if it were a sacred text,
transcribed word of some divinity;
        I didn't know the language
I was copying, was unsure even
        of the script, whether it was
a deeply unfamiliar cursive
        or an altogether alien system
of characters; I copied as if copying
        pictures, curves and lines

and dots that might be diacritics,
        might be the twitching
of a palsied old hand; evening
        work, into the night, under
the swaying bulbs; line after line,
        page after page, the freight
cars rattling world
        without end

90.

Tenacious winter's leavetaking, the sweet
showers continue bracing, cold.
I remember no recent falls, but my limbs
feel one large, tender bruise.
Somewhere off in the darkness
a bird is making noise,
a song I can't identify, match
to species, much less
to individual. *Bird*
is that thing that flies,
that sings, as *Plant*
is that which bursts
green or into flower
in the spring,
at which I stand aghast
or ruthlessly prune.
Among the cherry blossoms
in the park straddling the brook,
hundreds of pedestrians,
their voices a cross-conference
of Urdu, Spanish, Hindi, English,
Japanese. Bridesmaids smile
for photographers before the pale-pink
cascades, a hugely pregnant
woman embraces her turbaned husband
for the camera, two pairs
of baby shoes displayed against
the man's broad back. I know

these cherry blossoms by the Department
        of Parks's sign. Pear or even apple
would strike my uninstructed eye
        the same. Uneasy in a crowd.
Slush of petals in the grass, on the pavement,
        from the nameless bracing rain.

Something happened, something important,
in those last four minutes. I was drowsy,
loggy from a heavy meal, and while it was
the latest episode, only forty-five minutes
and self-contained, and the actors had taken
subtly new hairstyles, added new twisrs
to their familiar turns, before I knew it
I was watching the close, and whatever
had happened happened without me.
I'll play it again, he said, *but I can't*
play it the same way. Which is quite
alright, which is the way of the world.
You never forget your first, they say—but
I can't remember my first beer
of any sort. Can never hear that same
song again, no matter how often
you hit replay: the ambient
sounds are different, different birds
are singing outside, and you're not
the same person as ten minutes ago.

The music is digression, flashback,
data-dump. The music is anamnesis,
reminds us of what we already knew.
Who sings in the epic? Demodocus sings
to Odysseus among the Phaeacians,
before the twisty one, all a-blubber
with memories, launches into
the plot-turns and coils of his own
wanderings. Teuthras, among the rose-petals
of Capua, sings to quiescence
the war-hearts of Hannibal's fierce Celts
and Africans. Sings of Amphion, the Theban
walls, of Arion carried on dolphins,
of Cheiron tuning the ear of Achilles,
Orpheus quelling the flames of Acheron.
Aeneas sings too, to no lyre but the Latin
measure, and the pathos of his music
enraptures Dido, enraptures two millennia
of misty-eyed listeners. We listened,
        we listen, tried to count out
the bars and find the One—
        the tempo kept shifting, ebbing,
quicker then slower, rain pattered
        on the surface of the snare,
petals blowing and falling
        like flakes on the tangled cords
and haphazardly laid-out
        pedals. Pink petals on wet, black,
scuffed, or factory-shiny neon

pedals, fathoms of reverb or
envelope quacking, echoing the ducks
across the rippled pond. I needed
batteries, I needed a power
strip. Needed an electrified
lyre or a flat-backed baglama.
I needed feathers and wax, fairy
flying dust, at very least
an umbrella, a tarp to shelter
the gear. The rain was centripetal,
all falling in one direction, down
on the One. I'd lost the beat
in that four minutes, fumbled
the stream. Bluetooth to my headphones
was cutting in and out, out
of sync. Was keyed up or keyed
down, unsure of which
was the right key, major or minor,
where the dissonance resolved.
The One was the key to the others,
key to some if not all
mythologies, key in which the twice-born,
twice-resurrected, blood-boltered
frontman was singing—blood on the kitchen
tiles, smeared across the horns
of that tuneless untuned white bass.
The bitter quinine of the One, the
tonic; sour dark beer, petals in its foam,
glowing in the afternoon sun.

91. *The Backfill of Delight*

I.

Prevailing winds undue providence
unconscious oblate occasion gnomon
or whether better archive winding
trellise-like across sunburnt mirth
wild surmise unbuttoned grace
congratulatory over offerance substance
listening spellbound patient eremite
corkscrewed smoke crooking upwards
and the transfigured smallest branches
furred with pale green
blossom-slush fallen brittle
and rusty whose complaint
forebearance compliant glowing
warm no longer contagious wind
providence scant grace notes.

II.

Bare forked under superflux
blood-smeared horns stratified
whiteness no whiter for eternity
forms grasped foregone tree buds
and groping sunward bulbs
contagion blown aside to every
corner crumble of leaf-mould
forsythia bleached dull before
emphatic cherry blossom little
sparrows' intent conference enwoven
enraptured over new-laid stone

yesterday's buff over-emphatic sand
laid by last night's showers
crumbs of petals dried scum
rapturous distant compliance.

III.

Dumb compliant submission
brickwork unwitting new-laid ivy
reclaiming epicurean restrain creepers
restraint distant covetousness of barely
known object the recorded voice
clear confident restricted desire
conference of wings waxen weathers
fiddlehead involved woven curls
carved engrave curved lines
across staves fading counterpoint
avian conversation crossing lines
prerecorded hedged in improvising
against providence future unwritten
in the dim damp fringes beneath
white shoulders tides unseen.

IV.

Blindsided scrape roseate bulb swelling
insofar as blondness sweet fringe
proclaimed benefits half-pay withheld
four principes five perhaps a year's
dizzy span the same republican
rhetoric as if the case hadn't altered

model degeneration twilight dances
flare-up gloaming sparks carried aloft
fanned on wax wings sparkling pixie
dusted blown-sided scraped can't
find my way descending bassline
pedal point void in effect postage-
stamp palimpsest case altered
year's empty span to stow besides
coarsening of the skin and palate.

V.

Rerecorded adolescent anthems
anomie misplaced but appropriate
records postage-stamp fritters
scabs from sarcophagi mouths
whitened Père Lachaise heat
Coniston chilly sun dull baking
streets blindsided gloaming
calmative zephyrs implacable
resolve not joy no never too much
hilaritas a stoic excess rooted
in the same dead-end vision
anthem renewed transposed
to an older key fumbling
for resolution but satisfied
in the backfill of delight.

VI.

Resolved solution joyful as ever
to dull rictus grinning
Ishmael desert of icons grimace
half-brother seraph grapple
seize inappropriate hold
remixed masters vaulted apse
forty-three minutes modular
sketches out succession nothing
succeeds dull backing sequencer
irrelevant bacchic dancefloor
flashing pavers of the fabulous
artificer wax and feathers
museum'd among beaux arts
platitudes true after all
anomie appropriate but declassé.

VII.

Teenbeat tyger beat blaze
unavoidable eyes that which
in which communicant vessels
auricular public whited sepulchers
wastes of grey delicate even
evanescent washed away coats
egg-tempered timed luminous
light as limbs stirring backbrain
communicating across principalities
dominant powers dust of icons
migrating deity theft lightning

fertilities shiny nodding plumes
of desire backswing of delight
stoic excessive indulge informs
shifting light on casual limbs.

VIII.

Half-steps descending pernicious
bluster and sprinkle unsent
images unseen vegetative metaphors
cross-purposes quotidien collaborate
backfill of pleasure ever self-loathing
foraying grackles backdated greening
resurge again anew green
redundancy mocking frame's ache
skin's slough blue if not outright
despondent vegetable metaphors
unsent temptation serpent Kadmos
accepting the ambulatory cruel
joke on the serpentine whether
canal or boundary wall foul
or fair weather in abeyance.

IX.

Emergent residual form stains lilac
magnolia azalea chemical properties
province of the eye flowering properly
decorous formal provincial suburban
baize croquet mission furniture
shrubberies adrift proximate crockets

proprietory magnificence attest
documentary testament perambulator
parkside snow of blossoms rattle
of snare backbeat attenuate numbs
digits and the counters clicking
rolling over tyger blaze leopard
unprintable honorific effaced
damnatio memoriae scraped clean
of numbers and patronymic.

X.

Form fully formed perfect headsprung
primeval Athena-like elaborated
syllabary syntax dusting of empire
providence birdsong daily break tell
him yourself how degenerate his son
frieze of clouds revenant avian
conference transforming inwardness
to *epos* evanescent story by story
no principle of selection consecrate
blindsided by volubility scope
fair forms blighted mimic'd
blown out of proportion indignity
concede decadence breakers streams
swarm against pleasure's backswing
sullen sodden swiftly falling night.

92.

We were in a cave of water, puddles
        beneath our feet, streamlets trickling
                down the walls, pools stretching
beyond us into the darkness. Whatever
        train had brought us here—we couldn't
                remember—was long gone, gone
beyond memory, details lost.
        A little phosphorescent glow from some
                of the stones around and above us.
When we flashed our phones into the pools
        tiny fish darted away
                from the unfamiliar, intrusive light.
We were supposed to be the light, sing
        a hymn to the light. Little shards of sparks,
                little phosphorescent stones
in our bellies, wedged painfully between
        our ribs, supposed to glow through our thinning
                skins. Some books said the One had broken
into a myriad of sparks, whirled up in the campfire,
        and each of these sparks was one of us,
                or in one of us. Some believed that;
I wasn't sure. Darker and darker, my phone
        was at 2%, the hands on my wristwatch
                no longer luminous, and the little
white stones, with their comforting glow,
        rarer and rarer. It was Jules Verne
                without the wonder, a slow dub

on the car radio, the station slipping
into static. The clouds opened yesterday,
just as the kids started their last
big number praising love and friendship
and so forth—opened, that is, to rain.
The columns, the grassy moat, the lavender
cascades of wisteria, all darkened under the clouds.
Something in the sound system shorted,
short sharp buzzing squall. Everything fell
silent, we looked for our hands, our programs,
for our folding seats and umbrellas, could see
nothing, only a cave of water.

Not so much a cave as a tunnel, its floor
damp concrete, walls and ceiling anonymous
industrial tile, white. Caged electric
lighting at regular intervals. It leads
from the parking lot to the beach,
umbrellas and small children, smell
of wet dog and coconut tanning oil.
It leads from the hotel to the downtown
shopping district, side alcoves of curio
shops, falafel stands, travel agencies:
cozy and warm, when the wind howls
sleet through the streets overhead.
It leads from *The House of Saul*
to *The Neighborhood Where Diogenes*
Pitched His Pithos, passing sites
of historical interest: the room where Constantine

made his Donation, the seminar tables
around which the Seventy-Two compared
final drafts, the bed where curvy Abishag
tried to squeeze the withered David's slingshot
back to life. It leads from the Port
Authority to Penn Station, crowds of newly
dead, bewildered, clutching fare-cards for Charon.
Catacomb, columbarium. Walls an unbroken
card-catalogue of niches, labeled and unlabeled.

Even when dry, the ground back here is spongy,
inches and inches of heaved mulch, splinters.
When you stir around in it—a spade, a hoe—clouds
of insects rise up, small birds, unidentifiable
flying things. The birds are singing, the insects chattering,
circling my head in a curiously harmonious
ancestral cacophany. Buried somewhere around
this spot, the GPS says, the parchment map
says, the voices of the flying things say,
that needful thing. Somewhere in the midden,
under the splinters and mulch, the black earth
alive with grubs and grateful forgiving worms.

93.

The weather shares out the century, raining
        chilly, overcast with occasional
blown flashes of sunlight. Or still
        and baking, sparrows and finches
hopping around all day, chirping well
        into evening. Exhausted disco
remix of a dull day, hungover sweaty,
        not finding the energy to put on
the shower. Forgot to start the machine
        so the towels huddle damp and sour,
semicircled in the dryer's belly.
        Not proud of what we've done,
which isn't surprising, indeed appropriate.
        I listened to Eno's "Becalmed," a sloppy-
drunk Alex Chilton live set, then left
        Sketches of Spain on repeat
till I couldn't stand the beauty
        anymore, or maybe the memories.
My Loeb Callimachus—printed 1958—
        has a frieze of little swastikas
around the dust jacket. Skinny muse,
        the poem as eating disorder.
Chisel it into big granite blocks,
        tossed out across the lawn:
THE PRESENT DISORDER OF THE SENSES
        IS THE GASTROINTESTINAL ORDER
OF THE FUTURE. Set that
        to the lyre, the barbitos, the buzzing

aulos, the dusty double bass,
        in blurred and humid elegiacs:

        Something happened. We looked around, compared
                what we saw to what
        we remembered—ads in old magazines,
                hall full of sepia photos,
        the grainy TV commercials—were shocked
                at the difference. What's left
        between the gross and the net.
                What you net in, what
        ropes you in, what grosses you
                out. So different, and nobody
        remembers it changing. All so excited
                over the new thing making
        life easier. We didn't use to
                connect enough. I want to
        touch your hand, feel your anxiety.
                My icon crops my anxiety.
        The familiar rabbit ("Nicholas" we call
                it, after a children's book)
        scrunches itself under a coffee table
                on the lawn, party's leftover.
        When they took off the car
                door, the damage was worse
        than initially thought. It's never better.
                Elegy is really a form,
        satire a heaping together, lyric something
                you imagine singing. Imagine singing.

Show me how to live, he sang,
but never quite figured it out.
The roses of Heliogabalus,
child-princeps fumbling among
his own unformed desires,
alternatives of openings
and penetrative power, crushed
under a shower of vagrant
blossoms. Smothered by history,
bleared under Dionysos' eastern
enticements. Flows from Italy,
from Spain, accents of romance
degraded Latin. Achilles'
degenerate son. The offramp
rears up in your headlights,
but you're unsure of the number,
the location. The roads here
like a plate of spaghetti, back-
curled and overlapping. The books
at first were atlases, graphs
of how it all related—each one
rendering the last obsolete. Now
you riffle through them, ignoring
the fold-outs and inserts, looking
for some coded message, some
encapsulated instruction manual
for a baffled and unfamiliar
virtuality. *Show me how to live,*

translated from Chinese to Swedish
and back again, in too-small type.

94. *Bluescreen for Jon Hassell*

To achieve the deep, shimmering sea-blue
I had imagined, I laid down coat after coat
of differently-colored glazes, over darker
and lighter backgrounds. I held the panel up
in different lights, at all possible angles.
I caught my breath at a particular hue,
a particular combination. The final
blue, sealed under the last coat
of varnish, annulled a whole universe
of alternatives, each its own
peculiar beauty: sapphire,
cerulean, Mallarmé's unreachable
azure sky—the blue of pilfered
turquoise, blue of a vein
in a milk-white breast, the
blue of your eyes in first
        grey daylight.

The sky mutes down stifling, as if
the rain were holding its breath.
Fragmites rustle, echo the surf
in another octave. Air conditioner
hum, scattered tentative birdsong.
Rubber rumbles the boardwalk.
The first sprinkles' pockmarks, impressed
on the opposite page. Compost
of trivia. Strata. Accumulus.
An unpopulated future casting
long distorted shadows

into the past, where no one lives.
I spend my days, into the little
hours, re-reading, trying to make
sense of the old inscriptions—
some of them anonymous, some
of which I wrote myself.
Half the Rosetta Stone went
missing, and I'd mislaid the shiny
oval rocks that sometimes made
stuff legible. High tide,
rain rolling up the beach.
High time, lived duration,
time dilated or compressed
on the pulses. *The men*
who own this city make
more sense.

Around the bend, over
the dune, the buzzing
stops. The breathy,
caressed, muffled, distant
horn falls silent,
microtones dwindled
down to nothing.
The sound has been
in my head almost
forty years, a sweet
tinnitus, now suddenly
gone. An awkward,

unaccustomed silence,
like that moment
at the party when
the record's run out
and all the simultaneous
conversations pause
at once. Back
to Memphis, Egypt
or Tennessee, play
him the second
line into a fourth
world. The buzz,
the hum of rapture
under our cracked soles.
And the humming stops.

95.

authorized vehicles only a u-turn
even successful will take us
a half-mile out of our way
from night broad *pied-à-terre*
prismatic headlights over the bridge
inky palisades fireworks punctuate
soliloquies Richard Rodgers Amphitheater
the smell of weed across the park
buttock-curves of a picked peach
impending disaster subsumed
in the camera's eye steady hand
dabbing varnish across gold leaf
mixing powdered pigment and yolk
scratching patterns and lines
the lawns become meadows
the meadows burnt-over
stubble fields express welcome
of key cards and paid comity
without at least a bare level
drafting skill all flamboyance
of technique counts for nothing
so repeat and repeat
scraping discarding in hopes
of something salvageable right

split, into two at least,
and no longer looking back
ironically; the jaded gaze
no more a tragicomic

mask, but the real eye
of weary age; we expected
so much, they told us
we could have it all, be
it all; and yesterday
and today find us broken,
split; a baptism
in the nearby pool, under
hand-made banners; in a plain
baptistry, smelling of chlorine,
confessing and lying with the same
words; I count lines, and pages,
and words, towards a total
I'll never see; faintly moving,
the week-old bat on the Cleveland
driveway, fur shiny and sleek,
tense and alert the tiny mouse
on the Cambridge sidewalk;
undivided life, unself-conscious,
like the lilies thrusting impudent
around every apartment awning,
the clan of white-striped skunks
dispersed across the lawn, rooting
under the grass for grubs and worms;
your eyes were as blue yesterday
as eleven years ago; my skin
startlingly pale beneath the razor;
clouds over the reservoir
throw back the city lights

from their undercarriage, belly,
whatever, the towers still glow
through the mist, for now

On pilgrimage to Delphi, one girl,
passing under the Bridge of Sighs

in a closed gondola; the water sighs
against the prow, trembles

at a passing vaporetto. The steamers'
whistles drove Ruskin to distraction,

punctuate the paragraphs of *Fors
Clavigera,* punctuated already with myriad

digressions and second thoughts. An eye
ineluctably open to the world, lidless

and naked, flayed by vision. The girl,
quite rightly, will have none of that.

The gondola rocks, no hint of violence
or assassination, no Moorish revenge.

Turner painted his Juliet in Venice,
a forgiveable error, the bride-waif's

solitary beauty against the Grand Canal.
Lashed open-eyed, snowblind, to the mast.

The girl has outgrown Juliet—is a woman,
really—outgrown the oracles and catechisms

of yesterday. The palazzi bend over the canal,
the gondola eases forward, her eyes are fixed

ahead on Turner's light, on the Adriatic,
on Delphi where the podcasts end.

96.

Moon through branches: the sky's
soft grey, reflecting unseen city lights.
The fox is soldered to the sky.
I dreamed her busy among the huddle
of skunks out back. But the fox
knows better—is many-minded—
though the hedgehog knows the one
big thing that'll save him.
Are you, she said, amphibious?
At home that is in the air
and water both, bent over the block
and shaking vinegar from newly-
trimmed birch twigs? Too aloof
to make much sense, flitting
from clearing to copse. Cunning
vixen, timid rabbit, playful
squirrel. Their dark eyes
an uncrossable threshold.
A third of a thousand pages
of close and careful cross-hatch.

The twins upended astrologically
to an inverted *soixante-neuf*,
ready-made lickerish emoji
at hand: hands-free. Someone abridged
the sprawl of the Great American
Novel, removing its longeurs,
its philosophical ramblings, its passages
of descriptive stasis and becalmed
torpor: some clever conceptualist

printed an edition consisting only
of what had been removed
from that abridgment. That, dearest,
is the text of our lives.
Doves on the grass, moving intently
in and out of shadow. Last night's
lashing rain pools in the sunlight,
fills every visible container. The method
is Renaissance; the materials—titanium
white, DuPont's bespoke blues—
are *absolument moderne.*

They called him—repeatedly—a word
that no longer bears printing, whose open
sounding registers four hundred
years' poisoned humiliation. Smashed
his head with a fire extinguisher butt,
gouged at his eyes. We saw it ourselves,
justice's blithe or blind affection
for alcohol. Wood-alcohol blindness.
Epidemiological graphs and charts,
signs of the zodiac laid out
as indices of distemper, regional
and local fistulas. The port leaks,
the body's supple curves begin
to unravel, unweave themselves.
The caryatids' features, stoic, blur
in the acid rain. The socket's rim
presses itself forward around the still-
wet eye. The vixen's nimble cunning

is unperturbed; nor do the does notice
the running sores across their flanks.
Consider the lilies. Consider the pillar
of ivory, pillar of salt. Taste
of salt on the tongue, pungent
after-scent under the nails. Odor
a looking backwards, blindfold
vision. Well-fed and rouged,
Algernon's angels of instruction,
their chastisements a pendant
to his chastity, impregnable
tower of ivory. An innocent game
to play out in gathering twilight.
The vixen knows the skunk
is near, even at a week's distance.
Unaware, the does browse
their pointed chemical salad,
swallow with relish their sterility.
My life—a series of omitted
redundancies, struck-out punctuation,
of course-s, *that is to say*-s, crowd
of adverbs, press of ellipses.
The zodiac is a mood-ring,
a leisure suit; a macramé planter,
a session of transactional analysis;
Bo Derek's cornrows, Lou Reed's
aviators; a silver cocaine spoon,
the lettering on the cover of CREEM.
We will be sorted, one day, by signs—

the pierced with the pierced, waxed
and inked likewise. The patient
Zenodotus, weighing and choosing
the correct hexameter phrase,
sorting the miscellaneous scrolls
into novel pigeon-holes that still
determine our paths. No royal road
to geometry, or anywhere else.
Matrilineal patience pieces together
a quilt of dazzling polychromatic
double-knit: it will go up in a *whoosh*
at the first dropped cigarette, far
faster than the stacked and labeled rolls.
As if it dropped from the tree,
that bird—righting itself just
as it alights on the grass.
Back in Florida, a sudden cold
front snapped the iguanas—some,
three or four feet long—into hibernation.
As they sprawled on the ground,
smaller, warm-blooded beasts
scooped out their eyes and soft
viscera: leathery orange and ochre
bodies, slashed like ribbons all
across the grass. The zodiac turns:
the Year of the Dragon gives way
to the Year of the Rat.
Behind the branches, the evening sky
is a startling fin-de-siècle

mauve, color of an anime
pony, a sixteen-year-old's
hair, double-knit quilted triangle,
a new and livid bruise.

97. *Quest Romance*

Your boots, you said, were flowered
and androgynous, named for both
a devout gambler and an Odyssean
itch. You'd draw them on, lace them up,
and every day embark on a new quest:
to the park, the museum, the bodega,
every outing scripted in advance, mapped
in eternity. Footwear in dialogue
with an underworld of queers
and skinheads, skankers and dub
enthusiasts, habitués of the mosh
pit and the absinthe bar. Andrew
Lang had nothing on the Green
Fairy pouring water over your sugar cubes,
my dear, though the sweetness
sometimes failed to mask the bitter
wormwood, cloyed at the corner
of your lips. A new mystery at every
turning alleyway, pungent new strain
threading each billow of yellowy fog.

Where did those careful, halting sessions
lead us—though we'd agreed at the outset
that this analysis wouldn't be marked
"terminable"? No debriefing in the belly
of a throbbing Chinook, or uncomfortable
in a Chippendale before the big one's chair.
No tell-all memoir dictated hungover
to a chipper, enthusiastic post-graduate

specter. It would end someday, but never
give us the satisfaction of actually concluding.

A bicycle passes in the cool,
insect-heavy darkness. The voice
of a young woman, a girl:
you know what it is, honey?
I'm low. I'm drunk and low.
In the damp heaviness
of the room, my skin
is dry and brittle paper,
on the edge of blooming
into flame. The west
is already burning, the east
is spinning in flood
water. A billion insects
breed in newborn stagnant
pools. These twenty years
we've been living John's
Apocalypse—the Tarkovsky
cut—crying out for the rocks
to fall and cover our shame.

The real professionals, you know, write
the introduction last, after they've figured out
how the epilogue will dispose of the bodies,
where the celebrants and mourners disperse.
The plot, I'm afraid, is always the same.
The boots are ironical, you said, commentary

on or send-up of a thousand generations'
footwear. Mr Ramsay's sturdy well-oiled
boots, careless as a young man
on the rocks, cigar angled jauntily.
The lighthouse for which he's sailed—
with Cam, with Peter, no longer
a little boy—was planned by RLS's
grandfather, whose ingenious designs
spread wider than his grandson's
fables, provided more real succor
to humanity. The boots pinch
the first six weeks at least,
and then you're broken in.
There are really only two or three
stories. *The future is written,*
she says, the bike wobbling
around a corner, *it's tattooed*
across your forearm, the blade
of your sunscarred back.

98.

One foot and then
the other, a bright falling
forward, the trunk renewed
just before the topple.

The future is written, they keep
telling us, not letting on
that it's just the past
in new, luminous drag.

Rising from the chair, an audible
creak: the machine, worked
hard and ceaselessly
over half a century,

beginning to seize up.
One returns to the Preacher,
gets reminded of the vanity
of it all. How often

must one read Ecclesiastes?
She stretches in the yellow hammock,
ears buzzing with the latest release—
blowing with change, with love?

Measure time in emptied bottles,
in the eyes of shy and curious
animals just at the edge
of the porch light, momentarily

fixed in the headlamp beams.
        The insects will hush down
soon enough, now there's a chill
        in the air, the slow burn

of the compost heap
        settles into cool hibernation.
Traffic piled up for hours beyond
        the bridge, the tunnel. No sense

of flight beyond the atrocious
        chatter of wheels and gears.
The future changes every time
        you refresh the page, calculate

alternate routes. A quest-epic
        whose goal rearranges itself
every go-round: level up from
        the island to an outer borough,

timeshare to beachhouse, suburb
        to damp and musty basement.
The dehumidifier humming in a corner,
        she undid her dress, drew down

his trousers, brought in
        a whole new humid season.
Hard at this distance to know
        what he was thinking, even

with inside information: impossible
        of course to know what
was on her mind, siloed off
        as we poor animals are.

Do you dream of angels? she asked,
        Do you ever wish sometimes
that we actually believed *in God?*
        Beyond belief no blasphemy,

there's no profaning a set of quaint,
        antiquated, barely-remembered
playing counters. The future, they said,
        was straightforward narrative,

unbending storyline from Point A
        to Zion, New Jerusalem.
The Kingdom of God, someone said,
        is within you: fuzzy preposition—

perhaps *among you,* which opens
        visions of conspiratorial shiver.
A bright white beach, unreal
        Mediterranean blue:

her brown skin starting out
        in a series of Instagram
posts, breaking the blue
        of the water, the crystal heat.

The leaves begin to settle down
        and gather in corners: the old book,
heavy, limp, and damp, tells my hand
        to find something to do.

99.

Van Helsing in the British
Museum kind-hearted sorrowful and sympathetic
ponders prophylactics and cures huddles
in a foxhole of papers
books bound periodicals reason's Dutch-

Tongued representative *your eyes alight*
fieldwork folklore the anthropological gaze
charm against the evil eye
visions of necromancy psychic readings
automatic writing the riddle puzzle

Web every scrap of talk
leads on to the next
weaves the nexus the spreading
web of speech that binds
and entrances us *I'd rather*

Talk and *your love language*
is touch isn't it fingertips
callused insensitive to shrink back
into gross and obtuse self-pity
vulgar Darwinism models generic structures

Complex social order neologism Utopia
pain in lower back but
that's at best displacement reddening
colonial logics onetime Maori servant
codes of hegemony hierarchies broken

Faint stink in the refrigerator
too late salty-sweet on my
tongue uncertain tied and raspy
the nature of the hybrid
Book of the Machines neo-Lamarckian

Active presence of queer failure
delightfully invigorating atmosphere imprisonment sequestration
insight and blindness ocular surgeons
divinely inspired to reveal natural
beauty eyesight to the blind

You talk about your woman
a menacing consumption violence God-given
dissecting his lunch medical touch
the hairy hands of rapture
gluttonous appetite no less capable

Of being reduced to outright
sexuality the sign on both
sides of frank affection thou
resolute angel at one with
me love's dove-wing scarce turning

Ingests the body of God
Angelo the fallen angel Angelo
the savior slowly ripened 'neath
the touch divine uncomfortable uncanny
blind eyes at the core

Of the uncanny displaced castration
loss of function terrifying mastery
a surface reading illogical violent
unaccountable inevitable fetishization of unseeing
female eyes affectionate and inviolate

We do not understand how
they know sense what seems
illegible o'er-scrawled with curious detail
cathedral alive with crawling detail
dismal gaze of enabled theory

Pure abjection nothing to recoil
from disruptive gendered spectatorship male
gaze at its most violent
voyeuristic uncanny coquette arranging herself
for the conquest Mirror Stage

Unable to transgress diegetic boundaries
one more transhistorical gesture falls
on unhearing ears another Parable
of the Talents viral communicating
healing touch Our Savior's miraculously

Regenerating prepuce infantile or senile
the incapacity of age daggered
into the eager crotch embittered
by skills triumphantly acquired over
years discrete horrors of failure

Race of devils of rippers
leather aprons dovetail forensic certainty
the modulations of Childers' prose
logics of realism of impressionism
inherently like all language political

Affectionate and isolate each alone
in their prison-cell proud damaged
second thoughts not the dialectic
but lacerating introspection we gesture
in the dark exchange images

Speech at an impasse ground
crunching underfoot wanton carefully curated
acreage cellphone thrust under grotto'd
crotch seed on stony ground
or sown among wayside thorns.

100. *Biographical theory*

I.

See how the leaves change, and fall! Hear
the birds, the traffic a block away,
the occasional airplane overhead. See
the wind scatter the shadows on the grass!

II.

We're crowding into the auditorium—
carefully, tentatively—to see the old story
presented yet again. We've seen it before,
heard it from our parents' knees
through our postgraduate days. We know
every twist and turn, know how
it comes out. This time, maybe,
it will set us free. At least,
there'll be the tepid comfort
of the familiar, stuffed animal
or fraying blanket, washed and rewashed
to a soft translucent web.

III.

It moves to one great idea. Or not.
It moves forwards, backwards, and sideways,
blindly, painfully. Still it moves.

IV.

They wrote autobiographies
in the third person, to distance the painful,
the shameful. The mathematician

called himself *The Functionary*, a rare
calculus joke. Joking about stones:
as Pepys preserved his bladder-stone—
extracted with unimaginable pain—
to produce at dinner-parties.

V.

Subject of the day: "Experiment in Biography."
If autofiction, then why not autoverse?
Or is it all—by default—autoverse?

VI.

Splashes of startling red, the maple
leaves wet on the asphalt. Cold fire.
They should move me. They should be a sign,
symbol of something abstract and large.
The path through the woods, sodden
from last night's rain, is particolored
with fallen leaves, with wan shadows
of yellow trees. My shoes were wet
by the time reached the clifftop
overlook—Manhattan a grey
sawtooth wedge against the horizon.
Unmoving, neither retreating
nor coming closer.

VII.

This tells no story. I have no story
to tell. Reduced to gesture, pointless pantomime.

VIII.

Hunting among stony records, running
down shadowy ancestors: the trail
goes cold in a couple of generations.
Or some trails go cold. Itinerant laborers
have no parents to speak of, prosperous
farmers boast pedigrees all the way back
to English earls, French kings.
So many names, doubling every
generation, to converge on this poor
forked failure! So much labor and joy,
hope and frustration, gone under ground,
their only traces left in the wrinkles
and quirks of one shy mammal.

IX.

Nosing among broken stones, hunting
for the proper inscriptions. Your smiling face,
under a crown of magnificent white hair,
came up on my feed the other day. Fingernails
go brittle in the cold. The animals move
nervously, quickly. Fingertips numb,
I try to fit together broken puzzle-
pieces of stone, to recover that magic
inscription. Valley of dry stones. A shop
in Nyack, where scores of thousands of books
are piled, horizontal stacks to shoulder height,
in no discernable order. The inside
of my head, where a timer's ticking

louder by the hour. Some animal
scratches in dry leaves.

X.

The biographer begins each portrait, we expect,
with a brief or detailed run-down of the subject's forebears—
their nationalities, their fortunes in business or war,
the beauty or ungainliness of their persons. As if
the subject, the head exposed for sculpting,
were no less or more than the culmination
of bloodlines, the sink where all that DNA,
that history, that karma, pools together
in a single unrepeatable amalgam. A cold
bright Sussex morning: grimly satisfied, Henry James
stares down the bonfire, feels a weight lifting
from his podgy shoulders as forty years'
worth of scribbled life dances from paper
into ash and smoke, rises up into nothing. I am
my parents' spawn, each day reminds me, each glance
at my daughter's elbows—so like my mother's—
each glimpse of my father's papery, bruise-liable
skin on my forearms. A Huguenot ancestor
was pastor of the First Baptist Church
in Piscataway—"Stelle," *star*, fixed
to Kentucky earth as mineral "Steely."
The smoke, rising, is a pleasing savor.
The star falls, and the third part
of the waters goes bitter.

XI.

See how the leaves change! They tell no story,
claim no ancestors. They fall, they sift, they return
next year: pleasing savor or bitter wormwood.

Notes and Acknowledgments

These notes are purposefully minimal.

59.

The "checkerboarded" five-line stanzas of this section should be read as separate units, one stanza before the next.

60. *Spinoza|Andy Gill*

Andy Gill (1956–2020) was a guitarist and songwriter, best known for his work with the band Gang of Four.

61. *The People of Tsīyōn*

I've borrowed the spelling "Tsīyōn" from Louis Zukofsky's "A"-14.

64.

The opening passage of this section quotes Daniel Defoe's *A Journal of the Plague Year.*

70. *Disconnected Remarks*

This section embeds an elegy for my mother, Nelle Walker Scroggins (1927–2011).

The final stanza makes reference to the Ethiopian singer Ejigyehu "Gigi" Shibabaw, in particular her recordings with bassist-producer Bill Laswell.

72. *Septuagint | Jubilees*

Tyrone Williams (1954–2024) was a poet and wide-ranging critic of both literature and music.

76.

This section embeds a brief elegy for the novelist and editor Celina Summers (née Harrison, 1966–2020).

78. *Language Lab*

This section embeds an elegy for my father, Herman Wardell Scroggins (1927–1998).

79. *Water-Cannons*

Though already an established arboretum by the middle of the nineteenth century, Longwood Gardens in the Brandywine Valley took its present form as a horticultural showplace under the ownership of chemical magnate Pierre S. du Pont (1870–1954).

93.

This section embeds a brief elegy for Chris Cornell (1964–2017), songwriter, singer, and guitarist perhaps best known for his work with the bands Soundgarden and Audioslave.

94. *Bluescreen for Jon Hassell*

Jon Hassell (1937–2021) was an American composer, trumpeter, and electronic musician who formulated the concept of a "Fourth World" music.

97. *Quest Romance*

Parts of this section respond to the work of poet Norman Finkelstein, particularly his sequence *The Adventures of Pascal Wanderlust.*

These sections of this sequence—still ongoing—were written between the beginning of 2018 and the end of 2021, mainly in Montclair (New Jersey) and Manhattan. I thank the editors who published selections (sometimes in earlier forms) in the following periodicals:

Fortnightly Review: Sections 76–78.

Blazing Stadium: Sections 83 and 84

B O D Y: Section 67

Section 60 appeared in the chapbook *Elegiac Verses* (Ottawa, Ontario: above/ground press, 2020). Six sections were published as the chapbook *Pest: Zion Offramp 65–70* (Ottawa, Ontario: above/ground press, 2023).

Deepest thanks to the readers, editors, and publishers who have come along on this hejira—among them Michael Anania, Robert Archambeau, Billie Chernicoff, Sally Connolly, Stephan Delbos, Joseph Donahue, Norman Finkelstein, Elizabeth T. Gray, Jr., Adeena Karasick, David Kaufmann, rob mclennan, Emily Miller Mlčák, Peter O'Leary, Tamas Panitz, Roxi Power, Patrick Pritchett, Jill Stengel, and Marc Vincenz.

About the Author

Mark Scroggins is a poet, biographer, and critic. He was born in Frankfurt am Main, West Germany, in the depths of the Cold War, and grew up in various places—Germany, upstate New York, California, Texas, Kentucky, and Tennessee. He now lives in Montclair (New Jersey) and Manhattan.

Scroggins has written or edited three books on the poet Louis Zukofsky (including *The Poem of a Life: A Biography of Louis Zukofsky*) and a study of the English fantasy author Michael Moorcock. His essays and reviews have been collected in three volumes, the most recent of which is *Arcane Pleasures: On Poetry and Some Other Arts*. He has edited a selection of the erotic writings of the Victorian poet Algernon Charles Swinburne and (with Jeffrey Twitchell-Waas) a selection of Zukofsky's uncollected writings.

Scroggins's first four volumes of poetry, along with a selection of previously unpublished and uncollected work, are gathered in *Damage: Poems 1988–2022* (Dos Madres, 2022). Portions of his ongoing serial poem *Zion Offramp*, underway since 2015, have appeared in *Zion Offramp 1–50* (MadHat, 2023) and in the chapbooks *Pest: Zion Offramp 65–70* (above/ground, 2023), *forage acanthus* (Bodily Press, 2024), and *obelisk absinthe: Zion Offramp 113–118* (Bodily Press, 2025).

www.ingramcontent.com/pod-product-compliance
Lightning Source LLC
Chambersburg PA
CBHW020330170426
43200CB00006B/328
* 9 7 8 1 9 6 8 4 2 2 0 3 5 *